To

....

From

....

Date

....

When
Jesus
Speaks
to a
Teen Girl's
Heart

Print ISBN 978-1-63609-485-4

Published by Barbour Publishing, Inc., 1810 Barbour Drive, Uhrichsville, Ohio 44683, www.barbourbooks .com

Our mission is to inspire the world with the life-changing message of the Bible.

Member of the
Evangelical Christian
Publishers Association

Printed in China.

When
Jesus
Speaks
to a
Teen Girl's
Heart

BARBOUR
PUBLISHING

With special thanks to "Coach B," whose
love for kids and teens is palpable and
who prayed for me as I wrote. . .

Girl, you have so many thoughts, plans, feelings, ideas, dreams, and emotions right now. And Jesus has a lot to say about every single one of them. You are His beloved daughter and cherished friend. He delights in you! He wants to speak to your heart in ways that you never thought possible.

Jesus isn't an impersonal God who observes your actions from some far-off place in the sky. Nope! He's the "always present, alive in your heart if you've chosen to follow Him" God who loves you and is as close as your very next breath! He is *with* you and *for* you—always.

Jesus wants you to know His voice. As we dig into His Word in the coming days, we're going to find out how true this really is.

Hebrews 4:16 (NIV) says: "Let us then approach God's throne of grace with confidence, so that we may receive mercy and find grace to help us in our time of need." Through Jesus Christ, we can confidently and boldly come before God's throne. We're going to learn what that means too.

Come along with me, and let's hear what Jesus has to say to your heart!

Your friend, MariLee

I Have Chosen You

Hello, My beloved. Did you know that I chose you to be Mine? It may be hard to believe, but the truth is that I chose you before the creation of the world to be My child (Ephesians 1:4) *and* My friend. I decided to adopt you as My own because I love you more than you could imagine.

You don't have to hide from Me. I understand everything about you. And I love you fully. I sacrificed My life so you could be clean and free, holy and set apart. My blood covers you completely. You don't have to do anything but surrender. I am completely full of grace and truth, and I want to pour that all over you. Will you let Me?

I've set you apart for a great purpose, and I have amazing plans for your life. You're going to have some trouble in this world, that much is true. But take heart, My dear one. I have overcome the world! I promise to be with you every step of your faith journey. It will be a grand adventure too!

When life feels hard, follow Me. When life is good, follow Me. I promise to work everything out for your good and for My glory. You can be thankful in every circumstance, trusting Me to take care of you.

I am faithful. I offer you peace and rest as you learn to trust Me with your life.

I delight in you.

"This is what I tell you to do: Love each other just as I have loved you. No one can have greater love than to give his life for his friends. You are My friends if you do what I tell you. I do not call you servants that I own anymore. A servant does not know what his owner is doing. I call you friends, because I have told you everything I have heard from My Father. You have not chosen Me, I have chosen you. I have set you apart for the work of bringing in fruit. Your fruit should last. And whatever you ask the Father in My name, He will give it to you."

JOHN 15:12–16 NLV

Important Truths

Loved one, there are some super important truths that I want you to know and remember all the days of your life:

- *You are beautifully and wonderfully made (Psalm 139).*

- *I know you personally. I know your name and even the number of hairs on your head (Matthew 10:30).*

- *I see your tears, and I count them. And one day I will wipe every one of them away for good (Psalm 56:8; Revelation 7:17).*

- *I planned when you would be born and where you would live (Acts 17:26).*

- *Every good and perfect gift you receive in this life comes from Me (James 1:17).*

- *I love you with a love that will never end (Jeremiah 31:3).*

- *I will never leave you or abandon you (Hebrews 13:5).*

My dear child, you are so cherished and important to Me. I want you to live every day of your life knowing this! I want you to reach out to Me and to know Me personally too. I'm never far away. I'm always as close as your next breath.

Have you chosen to follow Me? Then My Spirit is alive in you and with you always. You are never alone. You're My child, and I watch over you very carefully.

When you're feeling down or scared or alone, please remember these truths, My lovely one. Come back to this page over and over. Copy it down and tape it to your mirror. Know that I *always* keep My promises.

"The God who created the world and everything in it, since He is Lord of heaven and earth, does not dwell in temples made with hands; nor is He served by human hands, as though He needed anything, because it is He who gives to all [people] life and breath and all things. And He made from one man every nation of mankind to live on the face of the earth, having determined their appointed times and the boundaries of their lands and territories. This was so that they would seek God, if perhaps they might grasp for Him and find Him, though He is not far from each one of us. For in Him we live and move and exist [that is, in Him we actually have our being], as even some of your own poets have said, 'For we also are His children.'"

ACTS 17:24–28 AMP

The Mystery

I want to let you in on a big secret, dear one. It's a mystery that I've held on to until just the right time. I've sent clues throughout the ages, and everything points to the big reveal of this astounding truth: *Me. Alive. In YOU!*

Are you up for that? If you choose to follow Me, I promise that you will never be alone. It won't always be easy, that's for sure. But it will never be boring either. Life with Me—Me, alive and at work in your heart—is the grand adventure I designed you for!

I came so that you can have an abundant and full life (John 10:10)! The same power that raised Me up from the grave is what comes alive inside your heart when you choose to say "Yes" to Me.

I gave up My life to take the penalty for all your mistakes. You can now hold your head high before a holy God because I've got you covered. I'm the only one who can do that.

I give you the strength and power to live your life confidently, even during hard times. I want to help you understand how loved and valued you are to Me. I want you to begin hearing My voice and trusting Me.

Ready? . . . I stand at the door of your heart and knock. If you hear My voice and open the door, I'll come right in (Revelation 3:20).

This mystery has been kept in the dark for a long time, but now it's out in the open. God wanted everyone, not just Jews, to know this rich and glorious secret inside and out, regardless of their background, regardless of their religious standing. The mystery in a nutshell is just this: Christ is in you, so therefore you can look forward to sharing in God's glory. It's that simple. That is the substance of our Message. We preach Christ, warning people not to add to the Message. We teach in a spirit of profound common sense so that we can bring each person to maturity. To be mature is to be basic. Christ! No more, no less.

COLOSSIANS 1:26–28 MSG

Hearing My Voice

I want you to know My voice, dear one. Let Me show you:

- *"My sheep hear my voice, and I know them, and they follow me. I give them eternal life, and they will never perish, and no one will snatch them out of my hand" (John 10:27–28 ESV).*

- *Whether you turn to the right or to the left, your ears will hear a voice behind you, saying, "This is the way; walk in it" (Isaiah 30:21 NIV).*

- *"You shall walk after the LORD your God and fear him and keep his commandments and obey his voice, and you shall serve him and hold fast to him" (Deuteronomy 13:4 ESV).*

- *Does he who supplies the Spirit to you and works miracles among you do so by works of the law, or by hearing with faith (Galatians 3:5 ESV).*

- *As it is said, "Today, if you hear his voice, do not harden your hearts as in the rebellion" (Hebrews 3:15 ESV).*

You see? . . . It's so important to Me that you get to know My voice! I want to show you how to do that. Wouldn't it be strange if you called up a good friend, told her everything about your day, and then simply hung up? Wait! She might have some things to say too, right? It's the same with Me. I *love* hearing your voice!

But don't hang up too soon. I have some things I'd like to tell you.

The Holy Spirit says, "If you hear His voice today, do not let your hearts become hard as your early fathers did when they turned against Me. It was at that time in the desert when they put Me to the test...." Christian brothers, be careful that not one of you has a heart so bad that it will not believe and will turn away from the living God. Help each other. Speak day after day to each other while it is still today so your heart will not become hard by being fooled by sin. For we belong to Christ if we keep on trusting Him to the end just as we trusted Him at first. The Holy Writings say, "If you hear His voice today, do not let your hearts become hard as your early fathers did when they turned against Me." Who heard God's voice and turned against Him?
HEBREWS 3:7–8, 12–16 NLV

Talking with Jesus

I am God in the flesh. I am the image of the invisible God (Colossians 1:15). When you look at Me, you get a clear picture of God. Can you picture Me in your imagination as you pray? I created you and gave you your imagination for a divine purpose. I want to show you many things on this adventure. You don't have to close your eyes to pray and talk to Me. No. You can talk to Me *at all times* and *in any way*. But let's start here today. We're going to read My Word and talk about it together.

> *I looked for the Lord, and He answered me. And He took away all my fears. They looked to Him and their faces shined with joy. Their faces will never be ashamed. This poor man cried, and the Lord heard him. And He saved him out of all his troubles. The angel of the Lord stays close around those who fear Him, and He takes them out of trouble. O taste and see that the Lord is good. How happy is the man who trusts in Him!*
> PSALM 34:4–8 NLV

Close your eyes and picture Me. I am close to you. Now just quiet your heart for a minute and be still. What do you hear? What do you see?

Here's something I want you to know: I want to take away all your fears. Can you tell Me everything that is on your heart today?

Long ago God spoke to our early fathers in many different ways. He spoke through the early preachers. But in these last days He has spoken to us through His Son. God gave His Son everything. It was by His Son that God made the world. The Son shines with the shining-greatness of the Father. The Son is as God is in every way. It is the Son Who holds up the whole world by the power of His Word. The Son gave His own life so we could be clean from all sin. After He had done that, He sat down on the right side of God in heaven.

HEBREWS 1:1–3 NLV

When I Speak

I still speak to My kids today, child. Do you believe it? I'm the same yesterday, today, and forever. As I said to My friend Jeremiah, I say again: "Call to Me, and I will answer you. And I will show you great and wonderful things which you do not know" (Jeremiah 33:3 NLV).

As you learn to hear from Me, you will see that it always lines up with My Word. "All Scripture is God-breathed and is useful for teaching, rebuking, correcting and training in righteousness, so that the servant of God may be thoroughly equipped for every good work" (2 Timothy 3:16–17 NIV).

I want you to learn to love My words. It's My desire to help you understand them. If you're praying and you're not sure if something is from your imagination or from Me, simply ask Me. Don't stress about it. Trust Me. I want to make things clear for you. I don't want you to be confused; I don't want you to worry. If I want you to know something, I will confirm it by making sure you understand. You'll likely hear it again and again in various ways, until you know that it's Me speaking. Your job is to be listening.

I speak to you in *many* ways. I speak through My Word. I speak through songs. I speak through creation. I speak through other people. I've spoken throughout history, giving people special dreams and visions. Try not to put limits on My powerful

ways. (You know that story about Me speaking through a donkey, right? Read about it in My Word—in Numbers 22!)

*Give to the Lord the honor that belongs to Him. Worship
the Lord in the beauty of holy living. The voice of the
Lord is upon the waters. The God of shining-greatness
thunders. The Lord is over many waters. The voice of
the Lord is powerful. The voice of the Lord is great.
The voice of the Lord breaks the cedars. Yes, the Lord
breaks in pieces the tall cedars of Lebanon. He makes
Lebanon jump like a calf, and Sirion like a young wild
bull. The voice of the Lord sends out lightning. The
voice of the Lord shakes the desert. The Lord shakes the
desert of Kadesh. The voice of the Lord makes the deer
give birth, and tears away the leaves of the trees. And
in His holy house everything says, "Honor to God!"*
PSALM 29:2–9 NLV

19

For When You're Tired...

I see you, dear one! I see how hard you're working. I see all your hopes and dreams. I see your desire to belong. I see all the worries you carry. I know about the questions you're afraid to ask. Are you ready for a rest?

Come to Me with all your burdens and lay them down. Close your eyes and quiet your mind. I am here. I am close, and I want to speak to you. Can you picture bringing all the heavy things you are carrying and laying them down at My feet? I have all power in heaven and earth, and only I can help you find the answers you're looking for. I offer you rest and peace as you surrender your problems to Me.

Picture yourself heaving the largest burden you're carrying at the foot of My cross. Give yourself a few minutes to imagine this in your mind. I bore this cross to bring you healing and peace. Allow Me to lift your heavy burdens. How does it feel to lay it all down? But wait... Make sure you're not picking your burden back up! Stand all the way up, dust yourself off, and lift your head. I am strong enough to carry everything you've given Me. Let Me have it. Let Me keep it.

Find your deep soul rest in Me, child. Stay close, and I'll help you live freely and lightly.

Jesus resumed talking to the people, but now tenderly. "The Father has given me all these things to do and say. This is a unique Father-Son operation, coming out of Father and Son intimacies and knowledge. No one knows the Son the way the Father does, nor the Father the way the Son does. But I'm not keeping it to myself; I'm ready to go over it line by line with anyone willing to listen. Are you tired? Worn out? Burned out on religion? Come to me. Get away with me and you'll recover your life. I'll show you how to take a real rest. Walk with me and work with me—watch how I do it. Learn the unforced rhythms of grace. I won't lay anything heavy or ill-fitting on you. Keep company with me and you'll learn to live freely and lightly."

MATTHEW 11:27–30 MSG

Unlimited Greatness

Do you believe I can do anything? Do you *truly* believe it? If you struggle with believing, please take a moment to be still before Me, precious daughter. I understand your struggle. I know everything you're thinking. Let's talk about it *together*.

Take a deep breath and tell Me everything. I care about what you're feeling. I can handle all your thoughts and emotions. Make a choice to trust Me in this moment. Repent of believing the lies of this world. Then turn to Me so your sins will be wiped clean and I can refresh you (Acts 3:19). Confess the ways that you've put limits on what I can do. Confess any other sin that is getting in the way of our relationship. I will forgive you and help you learn to trust in My unlimited greatness. Take a few moments right now and tell Me about your struggles. Are there any lies you're still believing about who I am and what I can do?

I want to refresh you and show Myself to you in new and amazing ways! Have faith, dear one. Faith is the confidence of what you hope for and the assurance of what you do not see (Hebrews 11:1). Without faith, it's impossible to please Me. So come to Me. Believe that I can do anything, and I will reward you for it (Hebrews 11:6)!

For this reason I kneel before the Father, from whom
every family in heaven and on earth derives its name.
I pray that out of his glorious riches he may strengthen you
with power through his Spirit in your inner being, so that
Christ may dwell in your hearts through faith. And I pray
that you, being rooted and established in love, may have
power, together with all the Lord's holy people, to grasp
how wide and long and high and deep is the love of Christ,
and to know this love that surpasses knowledge—that
you may be filled to the measure of all the fullness of God.
Now to him who is able to do immeasurably more than all
we ask or imagine, according to his power that is at work
within us, to him be glory in the church and in Christ Jesus
throughout all generations, for ever and ever! Amen.
EPHESIANS 3:14–21 NIV

My Spirit in You

Daughter, I have given you everything you need to live a godly life (2 Peter 1:3). I promised My followers that I would send a helper, and I kept My promise. You have My very own Spirit alive in you, reminding you of everything I want you to know: "The Helper, the Holy Spirit, whom the Father will send in my name, he will teach you all things and bring to your remembrance all that I have said to you" (John 14:26 ESV).

When you don't know what or how to pray, I will help you (Romans 8:26). When you're feeling stuck, lift your heart to Me and I will help. My Holy Spirit is your counselor, teacher, comforter, convicter, and guide.

Conviction happens when My Spirit pricks your heart about something that does not line up with My will for you. My conviction is clean. This means I don't want you wallowing in shame and self-pity. As you'll see in Romans 2:4, it's My loving-kindness that draws you to repent and come to Me. Ask Me to shine My light on any sin in your life, and I will do it. Confess it. Bring it into the light, and I will cleanse you.

My Spirit will guide you and help you do the right thing. You don't have to exhaust yourself trying to be perfect all the time. Let Me fill you with My presence, and I'll give you all the strength and energy you need to be the young woman I created you to be.

"If you love Me, you will do what I say. Then I will ask My Father and He will give you another Helper. He will be with you forever. He is the Spirit of Truth. The world cannot receive Him. It does not see Him or know Him. You know Him because He lives with you and will be in you. I will not leave you without help as children without parents. I will come to you. In a little while the world will see Me no more. You will see Me. Because I live, you will live also. When that day comes, you will know that I am in My Father. You will know that you are in Me. You will know that I am in you. The one who loves Me is the one who has My teaching and obeys it. My Father will love whoever loves Me. I will love him and will show Myself to him."

JOHN 14:15–21 NLV

Seek Me and Find Me

Let Me ask you a question, dear one: Have you been forgetting to bring all your thoughts and feelings to Me for help? Have you been trying to get your needs met from your friends, your family, or your phone?

James 4:2 (NIV) says: "You do not have because you do not ask God." I want to give you a gentle reminder today. I created everything. I have unlimited power to bless you. I know exactly what your heart needs. Will you choose to come to Me first? I want to hear everything about you. I want to talk to you. I want to answer your questions about life. "You will seek me and find me when you seek me with all your heart" (Jeremiah 29:13 NIV).

What do we need to discuss today, My friend? I'm ready to listen, and I'm also ready to help. Take a minute now and tell Me what's on your mind. What do you need in this moment? What has you concerned or scared? Let's talk about it.

I'm not playing games with you. I won't ever do that. I want you to seek Me and find Me. I promise that you can know Me and have a real-life relationship with Me. I will help you get into a rhythm of coming to Me for everything, if you are willing. Seek Me with your whole heart, and I will be found by you.

"So I say to you: Ask and it will be given to you; seek and you will find; knock and the door will be opened to you. For everyone who asks receives; the one who seeks finds; and to the one who knocks, the door will be opened. Which of you fathers, if your son asks for a fish, will give him a snake instead? Or if he asks for an egg, will give him a scorpion? If you then, though you are evil, know how to give good gifts to your children, how much more will your Father in heaven give the Holy Spirit to those who ask him!"

LUKE 11:9–13 NIV

Surrender

You can trust that I'm good. I see things from all sides and from every angle. You cannot know all My infinite ways. But you can know My heart for you.

Get into the habit of praying this prayer to Me: "Not my will, Lord, but Yours."

Can you trust Me enough to do that? I know you have so many hopes and dreams and desires. These things come from Me, dear one. Your desires are there for a reason. The things that you love and the tasks that you enjoy doing are important to Me. And I want you to learn to trust Me with them. Trust My plan and My timeline. When I interrupt your plans or ask you to wait for Me, it's because I love you and want what is best for you.

What is it that you hope to do this year? What do you want to be when you grow up? If you hope to get married someday, what kind of husband are you looking for? I care about these things too. Let's talk about them right now.

Talk to Me as you dream your dreams and make your plans. I want to lead you. Now whisper, "Not my will, Lord, but Yours."

I gave up My life so that you could live a life of freedom and find joy in Me. Trust Me.

You can surrender your heart to Me, because I surrendered *everything* for you.

They went to a place called Gethsemane, and Jesus said to his disciples, "Sit here while I pray." He took Peter, James and John along with him, and he began to be deeply distressed and troubled. "My soul is overwhelmed with sorrow to the point of death," he said to them. "Stay here and keep watch." Going a little farther, he fell to the ground and prayed that if possible the hour might pass from him. "Abba, Father," he said, "everything is possible for you. Take this cup from me. Yet not what I will, but what you will."

MARK 14:32–36 NIV

Accepting Yourself

Dear girl, you are so beautiful to Me! You may, at times, wish you looked a little different. Maybe you've always wanted straight hair or smoother skin. But I designed you the way you are on purpose. Trust Me, dear one! I want to help you accept yourself and your body just the way I made you.

Don't be concerned about the outward beauty of fancy hairstyles, expensive jewelry, or beautiful clothes. You should clothe yourself instead with the beauty that comes from within, the unfading beauty of a gentle and quiet spirit, which is so precious to Me (1 Peter 3:3–4).

Can you try something with Me now? Get in front of a mirror. Allow Me to speak truth and blessing over your body today. Start at your feet and work your way up to your head. Thank Me for a strong body and for all the ways I've made your body miraculously able to work together. Thank Me for feet that get you where you need to go. Thank Me for your legs that are strong. Thank Me for arms to hug your family and friends. Thank Me for every single part of your amazing body.

Remember, I look at your heart. Your outward appearance is simply a custom-designed costume that I gave you for your journey on this planet. It is not who you are. You are My daughter. You are My princess. You are a temple of My Holy Spirit.

I want you to honor Me with your body. Let Me help you do that.

Samuel said, "I have come in peace to give a gift to the Lord. Make yourselves holy and come with me as I give the gift." He set apart Jesse and his sons also, and asked them to come to the gift-giving. When they had come, Samuel looked at Eliab and thought, "For sure he is the Lord's chosen one who is standing before Him." But the Lord said to Samuel, "Do not look at the way he looks on the outside or how tall he is, because I have not chosen him. For the Lord does not look at the things man looks at. A man looks at the outside of a person, but the Lord looks at the heart."

1 SAMUEL 16:5–7 NLV

Plans and Purpose

I gave you special gifts and talents on purpose. . .to bless you and to bring glory to My name. Second Timothy 1:9 tells you something very special about My purpose for you:

*He delivered us and saved us and called us with a holy
calling [a calling that leads to a consecrated life—a life set
apart—a life of purpose], not because of our works
[or because of any personal merit—we could do nothing to
earn this], but because of His own purpose and grace
[His amazing, undeserved favor] which was granted to us
in Christ Jesus before the world began [eternal ages ago].*
2 TIMOTHY 1:9 AMP

I am setting you apart and giving you a life of purpose. I thought about you before the creation of the world! I have wonderful plans for your life, dear one.

Take some time to dream with Me, My friend. What do you love to do? What are you naturally good at? Write these things down. These talents weren't given to you by accident! What stirs your heart in life-giving ways? Talk to Me and listen as I whisper My purposes to your heart. Write down everything you hear from Me about your purpose. I want to talk to you about all your plans and dreams. I want to direct your paths and help you find your way on the path of life.

For this reason I remind you to fan into flame the gift of God, which is in you through the laying on of my hands. For the Spirit God gave us does not make us timid, but gives us power, love and self-discipline. So do not be ashamed of the testimony about our Lord or of me his prisoner. Rather, join with me in suffering for the gospel, by the power of God. He has saved us and called us to a holy life—not because of anything we have done but because of his own purpose and grace. This grace was given us in Christ Jesus before the beginning of time, but it has now been revealed through the appearing of our Savior, Christ Jesus, who has destroyed death and has brought life and immortality to light through the gospel.

2 TIMOTHY 1:6–10 NIV

My Kingdom Is Near

Things can look so dark here on earth, dear one. I know how you feel. When I came to earth and began to preach, My message to the world was "Repent, for the kingdom of heaven is near." And it's still My message today: "Repent, turn away from sin and come to Me."

It's easy to get sucked into what everyone else is doing and thinking. But remember that I set you apart. It's okay to be different from everyone else. I put you in this world to be a part of My body along with My other friends. Working together, you all act as My hands and feet in this broken world.

I came to bring light in the darkness. And I put that light inside you when you said "Yes!" to following Me. The light inside you is *Me*, shining bright for a dark world to see. This makes you different on purpose.

Think about your group of friends. I want you to be a light among them. How can you bring My message of hope to your friends even if they already know Me?

Think about your family and your extended family outside your home. I placed you in that family on purpose. Pray for them. Listen as I whisper ways that you can reach out to them and share My light and love.

My kingdom is here—and you have a grand purpose in it!

When Jesus heard that John had been put in prison, he withdrew to Galilee. Leaving Nazareth, he went and lived in Capernaum, which was by the lake in the area of Zebulun and Naphtali—to fulfill what was said through the prophet Isaiah: "Land of Zebulun and land of Naphtali, the Way of the Sea, beyond the Jordan, Galilee of the Gentiles—the people living in darkness have seen a great light; on those living in the land of the shadow of death a light has dawned." From that time on Jesus began to preach, "Repent, for the kingdom of heaven has come near."

MATTHEW 4:12–17 NIV

My Name Is Powerful

Philippians 2:10 (NLT) says, "At the name of Jesus every knee should bow, in heaven and on earth and under the earth."

My power is unlimited. Are you beginning to believe that? I want to help you believe. In fact, one of My friends said that very thing to Me: "Lord, I believe. Help my unbelief!" (Mark 9:24).

I want you to get in the habit of calling on My name. Some people use My name in vain like it's just another expression or a cussword. I want you to know how powerful My name is and to use My name powerfully and wisely.

Are you in a scary situation? Call on My name, and I am there! Are you in need of My rescue? Call out My name. I'm here with you, dear one. Some of your most powerful prayers are simply "Jesus!" When you call My name like that, you are declaring My power over everything and asking for My help and protection.

Are you struggling with doubt? I want to be real to you. I want to show up for you in whatever way you need Me to. I will hold your hand. I want you to trust My goodness and love for you. If you are still having trouble believing, bring that to Me. Let Me remove any lies you might be believing about Me—anything that might be preventing you from accepting the truth of My unlimited power in your life.

I pray that your hearts will be able to understand. I pray that you will know about the hope given by God's call. I pray that you will see how great the things are that He has promised to those who belong to Him. I pray that you will know how great His power is for those who have put their trust in Him. It is the same power that raised Christ from the dead. This same power put Christ at God's right side in heaven. This place was given to Christ. It is much greater than any king or leader can have. No one else can have this place of honor and power. No one in this world or in the world to come can have such honor and power.

EPHESIANS 1:18–21 NLV

My Other Names

Do you have a nickname? What does it mean? I have a few names that I'd like to tell you about.

Some of My other names are Wonderful Counselor, Mighty God, Everlasting Father, Prince of Peace (Isaiah 9:6). Let's talk about why these names are important for you to know.

A counselor is someone you go to for advice when you need wisdom. Some go to a counselor out of desperation, because they simply don't know what to do. I can be that for you. I am the Wonderful Counselor. Full of wonder and miracles, I hold all the wisdom and knowledge you will ever need (Colossians 2:3). I will give you wisdom as you learn to come to Me.

I'm also called Mighty God. I am a strong warrior, able to fight all your battles. Do you need Me to shield you and protect you in some way? Do you need Me to fight for you in a situation where injustice is happening? Bring those problems and battles to Me.

I am also known as your Everlasting Father. Just like I welcomed little children, I welcome you. Can you picture yourself climbing onto My lap and letting Me love you like a good and perfect father? You are completely safe with Me.

Another name I go by is Prince of Peace. I made it possible for you to stand before God in perfect peace (see Romans 5:1–2). Let My names bring you closer to Me.

The people walking in darkness have seen a great light;
on those living in the land of deep darkness a light has
dawned. You have enlarged the nation and increased
their joy; they rejoice before you as people rejoice at the
harvest, as warriors rejoice when dividing the plunder. . . .
For to us a child is born, to us a son is given, and
the government will be on his shoulders. And he
will be called Wonderful Counselor, Mighty God,
Everlasting Father, Prince of Peace. Of the greatness
of his government and peace there will be no end.
He will reign on David's throne and over his kingdom,
establishing and upholding it with justice and
righteousness from that time on and forever.
The zeal of the LORD Almighty will accomplish this.
ISAIAH 9:2–3, 6–7 NIV

Strength and Courage

Are you a bold girl? Or do you struggle with insecurity a little bit—or maybe a lot? Don't worry if you don't feel very strong. I do My best work when you feel weak! My grace is sufficient for you, for My power is made perfect in weakness (2 Corinthians 12: 9).

That's a relief, isn't it? As you grow in your relationship with Me, you'll see that I did not give you a spirit of fear. Fear like that doesn't come from Me. No. I gave you a spirit of power, love, and self-control (see 2 Timothy 1:6–7).

So how do you become strong and courageous when what you really feel is weak and afraid instead? You put your hope in My power and strength. When you call on Me as the Lord of your life, you are declaring that I am your director, your coach, and the boss of your life. You are surrendering your will for Mine.

And when you are listening for My voice and walking in My ways, I will lead you in all the places you need to go. I promise I will thoroughly equip and empower you for everything I want you to do.

So that means (1) you don't have to worry, and (2) I'll give you the strength and courage you need to get any job done.

As I lead you along on life's journey, you can be strong and courageous because you've put your hope in Me (Psalm 31:24).

How great is the goodness you have stored up for those who fear you. You lavish it on those who come to you for protection, blessing them before the watching world. You hide them in the shelter of your presence, safe from those who conspire against them. You shelter them in your presence, far from accusing tongues. Praise the LORD, for he has shown me the wonders of his unfailing love. He kept me safe when my city was under attack. In panic I cried out, "I am cut off from the LORD!" But you heard my cry for mercy and answered my call for help. Love the LORD, all you godly ones! For the LORD protects those who are loyal to him, but he harshly punishes the arrogant. So be strong and courageous, all you who put your hope in the LORD!

PSALM 31:19–24 NLT

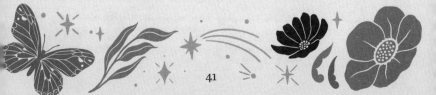

41

Giving It All You've Got

A rich man came to Me and asked how he could have eternal life. I knew everything about this guy, you see. And I knew how attached he was to his money. So I told him to sell everything he owned and give it to the poor. He went away very sad because he was quite wealthy. Many people during that time were under the impression that rich people would get into heaven easily because they must be blessed by God to have all that money. But that's not the case. What I'm always after is the heart. Not possessions. Not money. Not flowery words and prayers. I see what's in people's hearts. This rich man's money was a stumbling block to his faith in Me.

I'm not asking you to get rid of everything you own, but I am asking you to be willing to give up anything I see that might be getting in the way of our relationship.

Talk to Me about this, dear one. I want to pull you closer to My heart every day. I want to give you great joy that comes from spending time with Me. Can you think of anything in your life that's getting in the way of that?

If you want to give it all you've got in faith, let Me show you what's getting in the way. I'll give you strength to remove it from your life so it doesn't take over the spot in your heart that's reserved for Me.

"If you want to give it all you've got," Jesus replied, "go sell your possessions; give everything to the poor. All your wealth will then be in heaven. Then come follow me." That was the last thing the young man expected to hear. And so, crestfallen, he walked away. He was holding on tight to a lot of things, and he couldn't bear to let go. As he watched him go, Jesus told his disciples, "Do you have any idea how difficult it is for the rich to enter God's kingdom? Let me tell you, it's easier to gallop a camel through a needle's eye than for the rich to enter God's kingdom." The disciples were staggered. "Then who has any chance at all?" Jesus looked hard at them and said, "No chance at all if you think you can pull it off yourself. Every chance in the world if you trust God to do it."

MATTHEW 19:21–26 MSG

Love from a Pure Heart

The Christian life is all about love from a pure heart. When it becomes more about rules and religion. . .that is *not* genuine faith in Me. My friend Paul had some important things to say to his young assistant, Timothy, about this: "The purpose of my instruction is that all believers would be filled with love that comes from a pure heart, a clear conscience, and genuine faith. But some people have missed this whole point. They have turned away from these things and spend their time in meaningless discussions" (1 Timothy 1:5–6 NLT).

My goal for you as a young woman is that you'll be filled with purity and love and a real-life faith in Me. I know this gets more difficult with each passing year, especially with all the temptation and darkness online. My enemy tries to trip up young people any way he can. But My power is greater, and I have some tools that can help.

Before you get online, get in the habit of talking to Me first. Ask Me to cover you with My armor. You need the helmet of salvation, in particular, so that you remember that you are Mine and that you have the mind of Christ (1 Corinthians 2:16).

When you're in conversations with others or online, say quick prayers in your mind and ask Me to help you speak or post with love and wisdom. I want to help you steer clear of online arguments and meaningless conversations that cause division, hurt feelings, or gossip.

How can a young person stay on the path of purity? By living according to your word. I seek you with all my heart; do not let me stray from your commands. I have hidden your word in my heart that I might not sin against you. Praise be to you, LORD; teach me your decrees. With my lips I recount all the laws that come from your mouth. I rejoice in following your statutes as one rejoices in great riches. I meditate on your precepts and consider your ways. I delight in your decrees; I will not neglect your word.

PSALM 119:9–16 NIV

Why I Came

As you'll see in today's scripture reading, I came to earth for some very important reasons. I want you to know and understand these reasons. You will find them helpful on your journey.

I came to offer you freedom. I am the only one who can free your heart from the prison of darkness. And when that happens, you can live life freely and lightly (see Matthew 11:28–30 MSG). Do you feel imprisoned by anything right now? Maybe a group of friends, an addiction, or a lie you are believing? I want to break your chains and free you. Let Me help!

I came to bring joy and blessing instead of mourning and despair. Are you in need of more joy and blessing in your life? Bring Me your sadness and depression. Let Me carry your heavy load.

I came to bring beauty up from the ashes. Have you ever had anything explode into flames in your life? Do you need Me to bring beauty to something that seems hopeless and dead? I'd love to help.

You are My beloved daughter, and I am the King of kings, willing and able to bless you. I want to give you hope and bring healing and wholeness to your heart. You can face any hard thing in your life because I am *always* with you.

The Spirit of the Sovereign LORD is upon me, for the LORD has anointed me to bring good news to the poor. He has sent me to comfort the brokenhearted and to proclaim that captives will be released and prisoners will be freed. He has sent me to tell those who mourn that the time of the LORD's favor has come, and with it, the day of God's anger against their enemies. To all who mourn in Israel, he will give a crown of beauty for ashes, a joyous blessing instead of mourning, festive praise instead of despair. In their righteousness, they will be like great oaks that the LORD has planted for his own glory.

ISAIAH 61:1–3 NLT

Feeling Rejected

I want you to know something, dear one. I care about the things that make you sad. I see all your tears. I even count them (Psalm 56:8). They matter to Me. I want to help. Another one of My nicknames we haven't talked about yet is this one: "Man of Sorrows." Do you want to know why I was called that? It's because I was rejected by so many people, even some of My own very dear friends. I know how it feels—I know what it's like to feel alone and rejected. I'm very familiar with pain and suffering.

Whatever you're going through right now, I understand, because I've been there too. Are you feeling left out or not good enough? Come to Me. Your tears matter. Remember, My name is very powerful. Call on My name for help.

When you trust in Me, you don't have to worry about what other people think. I don't play favorites (Acts 10:34; Romans 2:11). You are just as important to Me as the president. You can lift your head high in any room and in every situation, simply because you are My beloved daughter—and I'm the King!

I want to give you confidence around others. They are not better than you simply because their jobs seem more important. You are so valuable to Me. There is no need to be afraid just because someone seems more important than you. You are royalty. And I want to help you to be yourself around *all* people.

But when I am afraid, I will put my trust in you. I praise God for what he has promised. I trust in God, so why should I be afraid? What can mere mortals do to me? They are always twisting what I say; they spend their days plotting to harm me. They come together to spy on me—watching my every step, eager to kill me. Don't let them get away with their wickedness; in your anger, O God, bring them down. You keep track of all my sorrows. You have collected all my tears in your bottle. You have recorded each one in your book. My enemies will retreat when I call to you for help. This I know: God is on my side! I praise God for what he has promised; yes, I praise the LORD for what he has promised. I trust in God, so why should I be afraid? What can mere mortals do to me?

PSALM 56:3–11 NLT

Don't Worry

What's got you struggling right now? I want to help. Let's talk about it right now, shall we?

Think about your biggest worry. Notice where you feel it in your body. Is it giving you a headache? Causing you pain in your neck? A big ball of goo in your stomach? I know exactly what you're feeling, but I want you to recognize it too.

When you try to carry all these worries on your own, it affects your body in negative ways. I didn't design you to carry stress long term. Stress can cause all kinds of disease. It can affect your health, your relationships, and your entire life. Will you trust Me to help you instead?

Come to Me. I want to exchange your fears and anxieties for My power and peace. All you need to do is ask and receive. Let's try this: Imagine we are sitting across from each other. I'll ask you a question, and you fill in the blank.

Me: Daughter, what do you need from Me?
You:
Me: Do you believe I can help?
You:
Me: Will you allow Me to help?
You:
Me: What scripture comes to mind when you think of this problem?
You:

Now pull out your Bible and locate that scripture. Write it down. Hang it somewhere you can see it every day. Commit it to memory. Allow My Spirit to bring it to mind when you call on Me. I don't want you to worry, dear one. I want you to trust Me. I am here.

Then Jesus said to his disciples: "Therefore I tell you, do not worry about your life, what you will eat; or about your body, what you will wear. For life is more than food, and the body more than clothes. Consider the ravens: They do not sow or reap, they have no storeroom or barn; yet God feeds them. And how much more valuable you are than birds! Who of you by worrying can add a single hour to your life? Since you cannot do this very little thing, why do you worry about the rest? Consider how the wild flowers grow. They do not labor or spin. Yet I tell you, not even Solomon in all his splendor was dressed like one of these. If that is how God clothes the grass of the field, which is here today, and tomorrow is thrown into the fire, how much more will he clothe you—you of little faith! And do not set your heart on what you will eat or drink; do not worry about it. For the pagan world runs after all such things, and your Father knows that you need them. But seek his kingdom, and these things will be given to you as well."

LUKE 12:22–31 NIV

51

Friends on the Road

Two of My followers were walking to Emmaus, right after I was crucified. They didn't believe that I had risen from the dead, even though they had heard about it from some of their friends. I walked with them on the road, but they didn't recognize Me until much later. They were sad because they misunderstood My purpose. They thought I would redeem them by rescuing them from government oppression. But I came to rescue people from their sins. I began to clear up their misunderstanding and shared with them all the scriptures that point to Me—from the beginning.

I decided to hang out with these guys a little longer that evening, and as I was praying and passing out bread for dinner, My two friends from the road finally recognized Me. You see, I'm the bread of life. Hungry people can come to Me to be filled. Broken people come to Me and find healing. Sinful people come to Me and are washed clean.

As you read through My Word, you'll find that every book points to a need for a Savior. Humanity has struggled with sin since that infamous fruit in the garden of Eden. I'm the only one who can make everything right and turn darkness to light. I'm the only one who can meet the deepest needs of the heart.

I'm glad we're friends, dear one. Come and let Me meet the needs of your heart too.

As they talked and discussed these things with each other, Jesus himself came up and walked along with them; but they were kept from recognizing him. He asked them, "What are you discussing together as you walk along?" They stood still, their faces downcast. One of them, named Cleopas, asked him, "Are you the only one visiting Jerusalem who does not know the things that have happened there in these days?" "What things?" he asked. "About Jesus of Nazareth," they replied. "He was a prophet, powerful in word and deed before God and all the people. . . ." He said to them, "How foolish you are, and how slow to believe all that the prophets have spoken! Did not the Messiah have to suffer these things and then enter his glory?" And beginning with Moses and all the Prophets, he explained to them what was said in all the Scriptures concerning himself.

LUKE 24:15–19, 25–27 NIV

A Reminder That I Love You

Today I want you to focus on My love for you. I have special ways to speak My love to each of My children. I say I love you through My creation, like the flowers and trees. Through My people, like the way I designed a mother to love her child. Today I want to remind you that I love you through My Word. The following are some great verses to write down and memorize and share with your friends and family!

- *The Lord came to us from far away, saying, "I have loved you with a love that lasts forever. So I have helped you come to Me with loving-kindness" (Jeremiah 31:3 NLV).*

- *This is love! It is not that we loved God but that He loved us. For God sent His Son to pay for our sins with His own blood (1 John 4:10 NLV).*

- *But God showed His love to us. While we were still sinners, Christ died for us (Romans 5:8 NLV).*

- *"No one can have greater love than to give his life for his friends" (John 15:13 NLV).*

And that's just a few! . . . My Word is full of evidence that shows how much I love you. Even if you've messed up more than you've ever messed up in your life, nothing will change the fact

that I love you. *Nothing* you can ever do will cause Me to love you any more or less than I already do.

Dear friends, let us love each other, because love comes from God. Those who love are God's children and they know God. Those who do not love do not know God because God is love. God has shown His love to us by sending His only Son into the world. God did this so we might have life through Christ. This is love! It is not that we loved God but that He loved us. For God sent His Son to pay for our sins with His own blood. Dear friends, if God loved us that much, then we should love each other. No person has ever seen God at any time. If we love each other, God lives in us. His love is made perfect in us. He has given us His Spirit. This is how we live by His help and He lives in us.
1 JOHN 4:7–13 NLV

I Was Tempted Too

When the time was right, I began My mission on earth. After I was baptized, I went to the desert and chose not to eat so I could fully focus on My Father for forty days and forty nights. My enemy, Satan, used that opportunity to try to get Me to sin. Satan is the father of lies. He lied to Me, and he lies to you. He will try every trick in the book to get you to mess up.

How did I combat Satan's lies? I did the same thing I want you to do: I told Satan the truth from scripture. But to do that, you need to know what My book says! Are you in the habit of getting into My Word and learning the truth? I'd like to help you with that.

When you feel like you are being tempted to make a bad choice, ask Me for help. I was tempted too, and I understand! I can help you overcome. When you memorize scripture, I will help you remember those powerful words at just the right time. That's one of the promises I made when I sent My Spirit to live inside you! Start with this one: "No temptation has overtaken you except what is common to mankind. And God is faithful; he will not let you be tempted beyond what you can bear. But when you are tempted, he will also provide a way out so that you can endure it" (1 Corinthians 10:13 NIV).

Then Jesus was led by the Spirit into the wilderness to be tempted there by the devil. For forty days and forty nights he fasted and became very hungry. During that time the devil came and said to him, "If you are the Son of God, tell these stones to become loaves of bread." But Jesus told him, "No! The Scriptures say, 'People do not live by bread alone, but by every word that comes from the mouth of God.'" . . . Next the devil took him to the peak of a very high mountain and showed him all the kingdoms of the world and their glory. "I will give it all to you," he said, "if you will kneel down and worship me." "Get out of here, Satan," Jesus told him. "For the Scriptures say, 'You must worship the LORD your God and serve only him.' " Then the devil went away, and angels came and took care of Jesus.

MATTHEW 4:1–4; 8–11 NLT

Be Salt and Light

In today's scripture, I'm reminding My followers to be salt and light to the world. What does that mean? Well, let Me explain. You probably keep salt on your dinner table, right? It adds a bit of flavor to food to make it taste better. And you already know what light does. So I want you to be salt and light to this world! I want you to shine your light and add the spice of your personality to a world that desperately needs joy, hope, and light.

You can share My love with others simply by being you! I want you to be the amazing person I created you to be. Use those special gifts and talents I gave you to shine for Me. When you do that, it brings Me glory and brings light to the world.

Are you still wondering what gifts and talents you might have? That's okay. I want to show you. Ask your parents or a wise friend what makes you special too. The people who love you can sometimes see those things even better than you can. Write down what they say, and then talk to Me about it. I want you to know how special you are and the gifts that you bring to the world. Remember, I have a special plan and purpose for your life.

Don't stress and worry about what to do next. Trust Me. I will lead you and show you how to use your special gifts to brighten the world.

"You are the salt of the earth. If salt loses its taste, how can it be made to taste like salt again? It is no good. It is thrown away and people walk on it. You are the light of the world. You cannot hide a city that is on a mountain. Men do not light a lamp and put it under a basket. They put it on a table so it gives light to all in the house. Let your light shine in front of men. Then they will see the good things you do and will honor your Father Who is in heaven."

MATTHEW 5:13–16 NLV

Words Matter

Do you have a brother or sister? Or maybe a cousin or close friend? Chances are you've gotten upset with them over something. Probably even recently! Maybe they were annoying you or not sharing the way you hoped they would. You might have even said something mean to them in the moment.

In Matthew 5:22 (NLV), I said this: "Whoever says to his brother, 'You have no brains,' will have to stand in front of the court." Of course, this verse doesn't literally mean that you have to go to court if you tell your brother he's dumb. But I am telling you that *your words matter*. Your words reveal what's really going on in your heart.

If you've hurt someone with your words, the best thing to do is to talk to Me about it first and then go make it right with the person you hurt. Don't worry. I'll give you the courage.

I want to give you My heart for your friend or relative. What does that mean? It means I want to show you how I feel about that person. Do I love them? You bet I do. Do I know what may have happened to cause that person to act in a certain way (maybe they had a bad day, maybe someone else hurt their feelings, maybe they weren't feeling well)? Of course I do.

I want you to be more careful with your words. They really do matter!

He who stays away from others cares only about himself. He argues against all good wisdom. A fool does not find joy in understanding, but only in letting his own mind be known. When a sinful man comes, hate comes also, and where there is no honor, there is shame. The words of a man's mouth are deep waters. Wisdom comes like a flowing river making a pleasant noise. It is not good to favor the sinful, or to keep what is fair from one who is right with God. The lips of a fool bring fighting, and his mouth calls for a beating. The mouth of a fool is what destroys him, and his lips are a trap to his soul. The words of one who speaks about others in secret are like tempting bites of food. They go down into the inside parts of the body.

PROVERBS 18:1–8 NLV

Be Trustworthy

People lie and break promises all the time in this world. It has become a common practice. Some even think that a little white lie can't hurt anyone. But that, in itself, is a lie from the father of lies.

Has someone ever told you a lie? It hurts, doesn't it? It makes you not want to trust that person anymore. It hurts My heart when My children lie to each other. I hate lying. It destroys relationships.

When I was giving My important sermon on the Mount, I told My followers how important it was for them to be trustworthy. It was important then, and it's important now. When you say you're going to do something, do it. Instead of always saying "I promise" to do something. . .simply *show* that you will by doing it.

When you tell your mom or a friend you're going to be somewhere or do something at a certain time, do it. That's called "keeping your word." If you don't, that person won't trust you the next time you say you're going to do something. Let your *yes* be *yes* and your *no* be *no*. Do what you say you're going to do.

I want to help you as you learn to keep your word. The more trustworthy you are, the more privileges and responsibilities you'll be given.

"You have heard that it was said long ago, 'You must not make a promise you cannot keep. You must carry out your promises to the Lord.' I tell you, do not use strong words when you make a promise. Do not promise by heaven. It is the place where God is. Do not promise by earth. It is where He rests His feet. Do not promise by Jerusalem. It is the city of the great King. Do not promise by your head. You are not able to make one hair white or black. Let your yes be YES. Let your no be NO. Anything more than this comes from the devil."

MATTHEW 5:33–37 NLV

Courage to Reach Out

Today's verse says, "If you love those who love you, what reward will you get? Are not even the tax collectors doing that? And if you greet only your own people, what are you doing more than others? Do not even pagans do that?"

This means that people who don't even know Me can be kind to their own people and friends. So what might I want My followers to do instead?

Well, have you ever felt left out? It doesn't feel very good, does it? I've been there. You probably know how it feels too, right? So let's help. I want to give you the courage to include others that look like they might be left out. I will help you be kind to them, even if you don't know them very well. Don't just greet your own people. Greet *everyone* around you with a smile.

Here's something to consider: sometimes shy people sit alone because they're afraid. Can you pray for those people to feel loved and accepted? I can give you courage when you're feeling shy and embarrassed yourself, because love makes fear disappear (1 John 4:18). Isn't that amazing? And I can give you the power to help other people who are afraid too. That's pretty cool when you think about it! You might even make a new friend and discover that you have a lot in common.

I'll help you reach out to people who need to see My light and love in the world. Your smile just might make all the difference in their lives today!

"You have heard that it was said, 'Love your neighbor and hate your enemy.' But I tell you, love your enemies and pray for those who persecute you, that you may be children of your Father in heaven. He causes his sun to rise on the evil and the good, and sends rain on the righteous and the unrighteous. If you love those who love you, what reward will you get? Are not even the tax collectors doing that? And if you greet only your own people, what are you doing more than others? Do not even pagans do that?"

MATTHEW 5:43–47 NIV

Prayer Map

I understand that some of My followers find it difficult to pray—especially when asked to pray out loud. Others like to make a show out of it. (They seem to be praying for the benefit of the listener and not Me. They like the attention praying a "nice prayer" gets them.)

I want you to know that praying is simply starting a conversation with Me. Here's what I told My friends awhile back: "This, then, is how you should pray: 'Our Father in heaven, hallowed be your name, your kingdom come, your will be done, on earth as it is in heaven. Give us today our daily bread. And forgive us our debts, as we also have forgiven our debtors. And lead us not into temptation, but deliver us from the evil one'" (Matthew 6:9–13 NIV).

It's a simple prayer, really. These words are like a prayer map. It has some important directions in it: like praising Me and asking Me for help and for forgiveness. You can add whatever else you'd like to the list. The important thing is that you're coming to Me and telling Me what's on your heart. I already know everything about you, but I always love it when you come to Me and talk.

You don't need a lot of words when you pray. You can simply close your eyes and let Me love you too. I'm not impressed with lots of flowery words. No. I care about your heart.

"When you pray, do not be as those who pretend to be someone they are not. They love to stand and pray in the places of worship or in the streets so people can see them. For sure, I tell you, they have all the reward they are going to get. When you pray, go into a room by yourself. After you have shut the door, pray to your Father Who is in secret. Then your Father Who sees in secret will reward you. When you pray, do not say the same thing over and over again making long prayers like the people who do not know God. They think they are heard because their prayers are long. Do not be like them. Your Father knows what you need before you ask Him."

<small>MATTHEW 6:5–8 NLV</small>

Let God Be the Judge

Have you ever walked into a place and felt like someone was looking at you funny and judging you just because of your appearance or presence in the room? Judging is when someone forms an opinion about you quickly, without knowing much about you or the situation at all. It hurts to be unfairly judged by someone else. But finding someone smiling at you with kindness can make all the difference, right?

Everybody seems to be judging everyone and everything these days. There are so many TV shows where judging happens—from how people sing to how they bake a cake or wear their makeup. Our society is trained to judge people.

But I want you to stop judging other people by their appearance. It's a person's heart that matters! Remember, the way a person looks is only a temporary costume for their earthly adventure. A person's appearance is not who that person is.

I can help you love people for who they *really* are, not what they look like. The next time you meet someone new, be kind. Give her a smile and get to know her for who she is and the gifts I gave her. Look past what she wears and how she looks to see the amazing person that I created.

Only God is the judge of people's hearts, motives, and actions. Let Me be the judge of a person's heart...and you just be *you*!

"Do not say what is wrong in other people's lives. Then other people will not say what is wrong in your life. You will be guilty of the same things you find in others. When you say what is wrong in others, your words will be used to say what is wrong in you. Why do you look at the small piece of wood in your brother's eye, and do not see the big piece of wood in your own eye? How can you say to your brother, 'Let me take that small piece of wood out of your eye,' when there is a big piece of wood in your own eye? You who pretend to be someone you are not, first take the big piece of wood out of your own eye. Then you can see better to take the small piece of wood out of your brother's eye."

MATTHEW 7:1–5 NLV

The Golden Rule

"Do to others as you would have them do to you." Hopefully you've heard this before. It's known as the Golden Rule. This rule has been around since ancient times—and most people, whether they go to church or not, have heard it and know what it means. It's really important to Me that you learn this.

The Golden Rule simply means to treat others as you would want them to treat you. This applies to friends, family members . . .*everyone*!

Think of the last time you were upset with a friend or family member. Were they treating you like you want to be treated? Now, think about the last time a friend or family member was upset with you! Were you treating them the way you'd like to be treated? If not, come to Me about this issue. Repent for your part in it. I want to forgive you for your unkind words and actions and help you make it right. I'll give you the courage to make amends and ask forgiveness from the person you hurt too.

It's so important to treat others with kindness and respect. To help with this, it's a good idea to get in the habit of thinking ahead when you are around other people. If you're having a great time but suddenly someone gets upset, stop and think about the Golden Rule. Is everyone treating each other the way they want to be treated? If not, ask Me for help to change the conversation and the atmosphere around you.

"Don't bargain with God. Be direct. Ask for what you need. This isn't a cat-and-mouse, hide-and-seek game we're in. If your child asks for bread, do you trick him with sawdust? If he asks for fish, do you scare him with a live snake on his plate? As bad as you are, you wouldn't think of such a thing. You're at least decent to your own children. So don't you think the God who conceived you in love will be even better? Here is a simple, rule-of-thumb guide for behavior: Ask yourself what you want people to do for you, then grab the initiative and do it for them. Add up God's Law and Prophets and this is what you get."

MATTHEW 7:7–12 MSG

I Am the Way

Let's talk about something serious today. You may have heard people say, "All roads lead to heaven." And many people think they're going to heaven when they die, simply because they're a good person and they've never done anything *really* bad. But that's simply not true. "I am the way and the truth and the life. No one comes to the Father except through me" (John 14:6 NIV).

There is a narrow door that leads to heaven—and I am that door. I am the only way to get to God. I am the only one who can offer eternal life in heaven because of My death and resurrection. I conquered death so that you could have life. No one else can say that.

There are a lot of people in this world who don't know Me yet. They don't know that I want to be their friend and change their life by placing My Spirit inside them. They don't know I can give them eternal life that starts right now. But I can use you to share My love and truth with them—if you're willing.

Your job is to love Me, love others, and be exactly who I created you to be. When people see that you have a real, everyday friendship with Me, they are going to want to know about it. You can help lead them to My door. I'm always ready to welcome them in when they come knocking!

"Go in through the narrow door. The door is wide and the road is easy that leads to hell. Many people are going through that door. But the door is narrow and the road is hard that leads to life that lasts forever. Few people are finding it. Watch out for false teachers. They come to you dressed as if they were sheep. On the inside they are hungry wolves. You will know them by their fruit. Do men pick grapes from thorns? Do men pick figs from thistles? It is true, every good tree has good fruit. Every bad tree has bad fruit. A good tree cannot have bad fruit. A bad tree cannot have good fruit. Every tree that does not have good fruit is cut down and thrown into the fire. So you will know them by their fruit."

MATTHEW 7:13–20 NLV

Build Your Life on Me

Ahh, a beautiful beach vacation. Have you ever taken a trip to the beach? It's one of the many wonders of My creation. I like to speak to My people through the wind and the waves, the warm sand, and the water lapping up to meet their toes. My oceans are filled with wonderful life and peace, but they can be dangerous in a storm.

If you've been to the beach, you've probably seen beach houses and hotels built right up on the sand. They have structures built beneath them to keep them from falling and collapsing during storms. Still, building a home on the sand is a dangerous risk. Even contractors who build homes on the beach warn that building a home on sand can be a big problem. If a big storm comes, the house can fall apart if it doesn't have a stable foundation.

I used this parable when I was talking to My followers about life with Me. Let Me be your solid foundation. If you build your life on faith in Me, then when storms and difficult things happen to you, you won't fall apart. I'm there to help you. But if you don't have Me as a solid foundation, you can fall apart when storms and bad things happen in your life.

I am the solid rock that you can build your whole life upon. I am the solid foundation that will keep you from collapsing in the storms of life. Trust Me.

"Whoever hears these words of Mine and does them, will be like a wise man who built his house on rock. The rain came down. The water came up. The wind blew and hit the house. The house did not fall because it was built on rock. Whoever hears these words of Mine and does not do them, will be like a foolish man who built his house on sand. The rain came down. The water came up. The wind blew and hit the house. The house fell and broke apart." Then Jesus finished talking. The people were surprised and wondered about His teaching. He was teaching them as One Who has the right and the power to teach. He did not teach as the teachers of the Law.

MATTHEW 7:24–29 NLV

Eyes of Faith

One day I was with My followers on the lake. Everything was going fine, and I even fell asleep. But suddenly, a big storm came up out of nowhere. Have you ever been on open water in a storm? I understand why My friends were scared. They were looking at the storm through human eyes instead of eyes of faith. The storm was a doozy. Waves were crashing up and over our boat. And My experienced fisherman friends were worried. So that says a lot right there. These guys were used to water and storms. But this one was furious!

Well, here's the thing: I was right there with them in the boat! I was napping. My friends really had nothing to worry about at all. But they were scared, nonetheless, and thought they were going to drown. They came and woke Me up, begging for help.

The great thing here is that they came to the right person for help! Only I can talk to the wind and waves and make them listen. So that's exactly what I did. The wind and waves obey Me because they know who created them. I hold the power over all nature. I always have, and I always will.

The next time you're in a scary situation, look at it through eyes of faith. Remember that I can calm any storm. Come to Me. I care about what scares you, and I have it all under control.

Then he got into the boat and his disciples followed him. Suddenly a furious storm came up on the lake, so that the waves swept over the boat. But Jesus was sleeping. The disciples went and woke him, saying, "Lord, save us! We're going to drown!" He replied, "You of little faith, why are you so afraid?" Then he got up and rebuked the winds and the waves, and it was completely calm. The men were amazed and asked, "What kind of man is this? Even the winds and the waves obey him!"
MATTHEW 8:23–27 NIV

My Authority

You've had a lot of teachers as you've grown up—including your parents, teachers at church, and teachers at school. I allowed all of them in your life to teach you different things at just the right time. You have some good memories of teachers and some not so good. But you can learn something from everyone you meet, even if you're simply learning how *not* to be like that person!

As great as many of your teachers have been, you know by now that they can't possibly have all the answers to your questions. But a good teacher will always point you in the right direction, right?

Now, imagine being taught by someone who created all things and really does know the answer to everything! Yes, that's Me. All authority in heaven and on earth has been given to Me (Matthew 28:18). This means that you can come to Me with all your questions. I have authority over everything that might come your way in this life. I am bigger than all your problems, failures, and fears, and I want to teach you Myself. Isaiah 54:13 (NIV) says, "All your children will be taught by the LORD, and great will be their peace."

If you've accepted Me as your Savior, My Spirit is alive in you, teaching you all things.

Let Me be your teacher. I am the ultimate authority. And you have access to Me and My power at every moment!

Jesus stepped into a boat, crossed over and came to his own town. Some men brought to him a paralyzed man, lying on a mat. When Jesus saw their faith, he said to the man, "Take heart, son; your sins are forgiven." At this, some of the teachers of the law said to themselves, "This fellow is blaspheming!" Knowing their thoughts, Jesus said, "Why do you entertain evil thoughts in your hearts? Which is easier: to say, 'Your sins are forgiven,' or to say, 'Get up and walk'? But I want you to know that the Son of Man has authority on earth to forgive sins." So he said to the paralyzed man, "Get up, take your mat and go home." Then the man got up and went home. When the crowd saw this, they were filled with awe; and they praised God, who had given such authority to man.

MATTHEW 9:1–8 NIV

Preparing for War

You're a daughter of the high King of heaven. And as My child, you have spiritual armor. You can read all about that in Ephesians 6:10–18. These are weapons I've given you to protect you from being sucked in by the thoughts and actions of this world.

Earth is a beautiful place, created by Me. But there is also a darkness lurking that can easily become a major distraction. Selfishness and personal pleasure are part of this darkness. I want to protect you from the darkness and temptations of today's culture. Can you picture yourself putting on the whole armor of God?

I put you in your world for a purpose, but I want you to be *in* it and not *of* it (John 17:14–16). This means you don't have the same value system as the people of the world—those who aren't following Me. You're supposed to be different, dear one! Being different is good. I want to give you courage for this assignment.

I also want you to learn to take your thoughts captive. This is a really big deal, My friend. You become what you think about. I want to give you supernatural power to take your thoughts captive. You are preparing for the war in your mind that affects everything you do. Taking your thoughts captive means that you are training your brain to take the impure thoughts that come to your mind and turn them over to Me. I will teach you to switch these thoughts to good thoughts. This takes practice and prayer. And I will help you!

The world is unprincipled. It's dog-eat-dog out there! The world doesn't fight fair. But we don't live or fight our battles that way—never have and never will. The tools of our trade aren't for marketing or manipulation, but they are for demolishing that entire massively corrupt culture. We use our powerful God-tools for smashing warped philosophies, tearing down barriers erected against the truth of God, fitting every loose thought and emotion and impulse into the structure of life shaped by Christ. Our tools are ready at hand for clearing the ground of every obstruction and building lives of obedience into maturity.

2 CORINTHIANS 10:3–6 MSG

81

I Am God of the Impossible

Let Me tell you a true story about one of My miracles. A church leader came to Me in a desperate situation: his daughter had just died. He asked Me to come with him, and so I did. As was common at the time, there was a crowd gathered outside mourning her death. They didn't believe in Me. They didn't know that I have all power over life and death. They even laughed when I spoke to them. But the young girl's father had hope in Me. He had begun to believe that I could do the impossible.

I took the girl by her hand, and she got up! To the crowd, the situation seemed hopeless. The girl was dead. What could anyone do? But the father trusted that I am who I say I am. He came to Me and asked for help, and I answered.

I want to give you faith like the young girl's dad had. I also want to take your hand like I took this little girl's hand. I love you, and you are so important to Me! Your faith in Me—the God of miracles—will make all the difference in your life. Believe that I can do anything. Trust that I want what is best for you. Trust that I can still do miracles today.

I am with you. I will take your hand in Mine. The impossible is possible with Me.

While he was saying this, a synagogue leader came and knelt before him and said, "My daughter has just died. But come and put your hand on her, and she will live." Jesus got up and went with him, and so did his disciples. . . . When Jesus entered the synagogue leader's house and saw the noisy crowd and people playing pipes, he said, "Go away. The girl is not dead but asleep." But they laughed at him. After the crowd had been put outside, he went in and took the girl by the hand, and she got up. News of this spread through all that region.
MATTHEW 9:18–19, 23–26 NIV

Simple Faith

Another desperate person came to Me once. She had suffered with a bleeding disorder for twelve years, and no one knew how to help her. She had spent all her money trying to find a cure. The doctors couldn't make her disease go away. She was labeled by others as "unclean" and was considered untouchable. According to Jewish law, I would be considered "unclean" if I touched her Myself.

So she came to Me quietly, through the crowd. She didn't call out. She simply touched the hem of My garment. And instantly, I healed her. This dear woman tried to slip away unnoticed, but I called to her anyway. Even though she was labeled by others as "unclean," she was precious to Me.

I wanted her to know that it was her simple faith in Me that healed her. I was so happy to free her from her long years of suffering.

Dear one, I want you to know this: I'm so glad you've decided to become My friend. Your simple faith will continue to grow every day as you put your trust in Me. Even if your faith in Me seems small and new, I am the God of miracles who can be trusted with everything that concerns you.

I want you to come to Me about everything that is on your heart and in your mind. Big things and small things—I care about it all. You are precious to Me. Listen as I whisper My plans and purposes for your life.

A large crowd followed and pressed around him. And a woman was there who had been subject to bleeding for twelve years. She had suffered a great deal under the care of many doctors and had spent all she had, yet instead of getting better she grew worse. When she heard about Jesus, she came up behind him in the crowd and touched his cloak, because she thought, "If I just touch his clothes, I will be healed." Immediately her bleeding stopped and she felt in her body that she was freed from her suffering. . . . He said to her, "Daughter, your faith has healed you. Go in peace and be freed from your suffering."

MARK 5:24–29, 34 NIV

The Good Shepherd

In the place I grew up, shepherds were a regular part of everyday life. I talk about shepherds a lot in My Word. Here are just a few places you can find references to shepherds:

- *"I am the good shepherd. The good shepherd lays down his life for the sheep" (John 10:11 NIV).*

- *He tends his flock like a shepherd: He gathers the lambs in his arms and carries them close to his heart; he gently leads those that have young (Isaiah 40:11 NIV).*

- *"My sheep listen to my voice; I know them, and they follow me. I give them eternal life, and they shall never perish; no one will snatch them out of my hand. My Father, who has given them to Me, is greater than all; no one can snatch them out of my Father's hand" (John 10:27–29 NIV).*

Why do I want you to know this? I want you to think of Me as your shepherd. A good shepherd protects, feeds, and cares for his sheep. When you stay close to Me, I will lead you to the right places. When you wander off, you can get lost, hurt, and confused. But I will come for you. Matthew 18:12 (NIV) says: "If a man owns a hundred sheep, and one of them wanders away, will he not leave the ninety-nine on the hills and go to look for the one that wandered off?"

Where are you feeling lost, hurt, or confused? Let Me be your Good Shepherd.

The Lord is my Shepherd. I will have everything I need. He lets me rest in fields of green grass. He leads me beside the quiet waters. He makes me strong again. He leads me in the way of living right with Himself which brings honor to His name. Yes, even if I walk through the valley of the shadow of death, I will not be afraid of anything, because You are with me. You have a walking stick with which to guide and one with which to help. These comfort me. You are making a table of food ready for me in front of those who hate me. You have poured oil on my head. I have everything I need. For sure, You will give me goodness and loving-kindness all the days of my life. Then I will live with You in Your house forever.
PSALM 23 NLV

Ordinary to Extraordinary

When I started My ministry on earth, I called twelve regular guys to come and follow Me. I didn't *make* them come. They had a choice. They became My friends. They weren't world leaders and didn't have a large following. They were fishermen. . .and one was even a hated tax collector.

Guess what I did with these guys? I used these twelve men to change the whole world. I gave them supernatural power to heal sickness and cast out demons. They spread My message all over the world. You and your family heard about My message because of what these ordinary guys did so long ago! I chose these disciples to show that I can use anyone. The same is true today.

You may not think that you have any great talents or gifts that I can use. But the truth is that I can use *anything* you bring to Me. And I can turn it into something that brings honor to Me and blessing to you.

I've got great plans for you, My friend! See what My Word says about that: "'For I know the plans I have for you,' declares the LORD, 'plans to prosper you and not to harm you, plans to give you hope and a future'" (Jeremiah 29:11 NIV).

Stick by My side, dear one. Friendship with Me makes all the difference. Even when you feel unsure about yourself and what you have to offer the world. . .My plans for you are good. I can turn your ordinary to extraordinary.

Jesus summoned His twelve disciples and gave them authority and power over unclean spirits, to cast them out, and to heal every kind of disease and every kind of sickness. Now these are the names of the twelve apostles (special messengers, personally chosen representatives): first, Simon, who is called Peter, and Andrew, his brother; James the son of Zebedee, and John his brother; Philip and Bartholomew (Nathanael); Thomas and Matthew (Levi) the tax collector; James the son of Alphaeus, and Thaddaeus (Judas, not Iscariot); Simon the Cananaean (Zealot), and Judas Iscariot, the one who betrayed Him.
MATTHEW 10:1–4 AMP

Speaking Up

I will ask you to speak up about your faith in Me from time to time. It's what I call My followers to do. We'll talk about something called the Great Commission later on. But don't worry, dear one. I tell you this so you'll be prepared and unafraid.

When I want you to speak up about something, I will give you a sense in your heart. Your heart might even start to pound a little. But again, this is not something to worry about. Why? Because right here, in our scripture for today, it says, "Do not worry what you will say or how you will say it. The words will be given you when the time comes."

If I want you to say something, I'll be there to help. If you submit yourself to Me, I'll give you the perfect thing to say or do at just the right time. And even if you feel like you've messed it up or said the wrong thing, don't worry about that either! I can take what you've said or done and turn it into something good.

As you grow into an adult, I want you to learn that you don't have to worry about any situation, because I am always with you. When you worry, you are imagining a scenario without Me in it. Come to Me, and I'll help you train your brain to seek Me first—before worry sets in.

"I am sending you out like sheep with wolves all around you. Be wise like snakes and gentle like doves. But look out for men. They will take you up to their courts and they will hurt you in their places of worship. They will take you in front of the leaders of the people and of the kings because of Me. You will tell them and the people who do not know God about Me. When you are put into their hands, do not worry what you will say or how you will say it. The words will be given you when the time comes. It will not be you who will speak the words. The Spirit of your Father will speak through you."

MATTHEW 10:16–20 NLV

Wonderfully Made

Remember that time you felt like you weren't important? . . . Like nobody cared about your feelings and there wasn't anyone around to listen to you? I saw your pain, dear one. And I have some things to say about that.

The psalmist wrote these words to Me—and they are important for you to know. He said: "For you created my inmost being; you knit me together in my mother's womb. I praise you because I am fearfully and wonderfully made; your works are wonderful, I know that full well" (Psalm 139:13–14 NIV).

I created you, dear one. I crafted all your body parts together and made them grow inside your mother's womb. You are wonderfully designed and created for a purpose. You matter to Me.

I know everything about you, and I care for you more than anything else in creation. I see you in every moment—I know that's hard to imagine, but it is true. There are billions of people in the world, and I still know you personally. I know your name. I know when you sit down and when you get up.

You are so important to Me that I chose to die a brutal death on the cross to free you from sin and take away all your sins. Because I did this, you get to be with Me now and for all eternity. The next time you're feeling down or unimportant. . .remember that I made you and love you. I am *always* here for you.

"Don't be bluffed into silence by the threats of bullies. There's nothing they can do to your soul, your core being. Save your fear for God, who holds your entire life—body and soul—in his hands. What's the price of a pet canary? Some loose change, right? And God cares what happens to it even more than you do. He pays even greater attention to you, down to the last detail—even numbering the hairs on your head! So don't be intimidated by all this bully talk. You're worth more than a million canaries."
MATTHEW 10:28–31 MSG

Blessing and Cursing with Your Words

Your words have the power to bless or to curse. What do I mean by that? Take a look at this: "People can tame all kinds of animals, birds, reptiles, and fish, but no one can tame the tongue. It is restless and evil, full of deadly poison. Sometimes it praises our Lord and Father, and sometimes it curses those who have been made in the image of God. And so blessing and cursing come pouring out of the same mouth. Surely, my brothers and sisters, this is not right!" (James 3: 7–10 NLT).

Words are important. Once you've said something harmful to a person, you can never take it back. You can only be forgiven.

Here's a few other things I'd like you to know about your words:

- *"A good man will speak good things because of the good in him. A bad man will speak bad things because of the sin in him" (Matthew 12:35 NLV).*

- *Instead, we will speak the truth in love, growing in every way more and more like Christ, who is the head of his body, the church (Ephesians 4:15 NLT).*

I always speak the truth, but I do it in love. I want to help

you do the same thing. And even if you need to have a difficult and honest conversation with someone, you can do that lovingly too. I'll show you how.

"If you grow a healthy tree, you'll pick healthy fruit. If you grow a diseased tree, you'll pick worm-eaten fruit. The fruit tells you about the tree. You have minds like a snake pit! How do you suppose what you say is worth anything when you are so foul-minded? It's your heart, not the dictionary, that gives meaning to your words. A good person produces good deeds and words season after season. An evil person is a blight on the orchard. Let me tell you something: Every one of these careless words is going to come back to haunt you. There will be a time of Reckoning. Words are powerful; take them seriously. Words can be your salvation. Words can also be your damnation."
MATTHEW 12:33–37 MSG

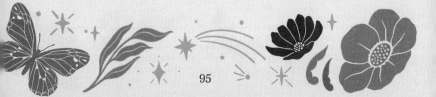

My Family

Family is important to Me. And I know that every person on earth needs one. It's true that some kids grow up without a mother and father, but that was not My design. Look at what Psalm 68:6 (NIV) says: "God sets the lonely in families."

When you commit to following Me and choose to be My child, you become part of My family—the family of God. Anyone who comes to Me suddenly has a world full of mothers, fathers, brothers, and sisters. I set people in families. I made you to be in community with other people.

I want you to learn from each other. You grow and mature around My other family members. That's all part of My plan for you. I don't want you to be lonely.

Being part of a family comes with responsibilities. It's important to care for your brothers and sisters all around the world. You can do that by praying for them. Pray for missionaries to other countries who spread My Word all over the world. It's also good to find a local church who holds strong to My Word and teaches truth. There you can share with your fellow believers and encourage one another.

If you are having a hard time finding good friends right now, I want to help! I care about all your relationships, and I want you to have a good church family around to help you in this life.

While he was still talking to the crowd, his mother and brothers showed up. They were outside trying to get a message to him. Someone told Jesus, "Your mother and brothers are out here, wanting to speak with you." Jesus didn't respond directly, but said, "Who do you think my mother and brothers are?" He then stretched out his hand toward his disciples. "Look closely. These are my mother and brothers. Obedience is thicker than blood. The person who obeys my heavenly Father's will is my brother and sister and mother."

MATTHEW 12:46–50 MSG

Seeing the Miracles

When I began My ministry, I traveled around to many towns and villages, sharing about the kingdom of God. I went back to My hometown for a while, and I started sharing the good news there just like I'd done everywhere else. At first, the people were amazed. But then they got upset and offended. They'd known Me since I was just a little boy! They didn't understand how I could call Myself the Son of God when they knew that I was the son of Mary and Joseph.

My neighbors didn't believe what I was saying. They couldn't look past what they thought they understood about Me and My Father in heaven. I didn't do many miracles there in My hometown because My neighbors didn't have much faith.

If you believe that I am who I say I am, then you'll accept all the miracles that I want to do in your life in the future. If you have a hard time trusting Me, you won't be able to see the miracles all around you.

Take a minute and think about your life. What miracles have you already experienced? Your birth is a miracle story! Let's start there. Write down the miracles as they come to mind so you never forget. I want to open your eyes to trust Me and see the miracles that I have done and *can do* in your life!

And when Jesus had finished these parables, he went away from there, and coming to his hometown he taught them in their synagogue, so that they were astonished, and said, "Where did this man get this wisdom and these mighty works? Is not this the carpenter's son? Is not his mother called Mary? And are not his brothers James and Joseph and Simon and Judas? And are not all his sisters with us? Where then did this man get all these things?" And they took offense at him. But Jesus said to them, "A prophet is not without honor except in his hometown and in his own household." And he did not do many mighty works there, because of their unbelief.

MATTHEW 13:53–58 ESV

Walking on the Waves

You've probably heard the stories about My ability to walk on water. Remember, I'm the author of creation. I can do things that seem impossible to the human mind. All the universe must submit to My authority.

When My disciple friends were getting to know Me, this blew their minds a bit. Let Me tell you what happened. My friends were out on the water in a boat. I simply walked over to them. This scared them out of their wits! They thought I was a spirit of some sort. I don't want My followers to be afraid, so I immediately told them that they shouldn't be afraid.

Peter saw Me and called out. He wanted to come out on the water with Me. At first, he had faith that if I said it, he could do it too. So I told him to come to Me. Do you know what happened after that? Peter took his eyes off Me and looked around. He became afraid—and that's where he went wrong.

Peter cried out to Me for help when he realized how crazy and unbelievable it seemed to step out in faith! I didn't let him sink, though. I caught him quickly.

Here's what I want you to know, dear one: when your eyes are focused on Me, I'll give you the ability to rise above the storms of life. Look at Me instead of your problems. Trust Me to give you strength and peace.

Just before the light of day, Jesus went to them walking on the water. When the followers saw Him walking on the water, they were afraid. They said, "It is a spirit." They cried out with fear. At once Jesus spoke to them and said, "Take hope. It is I. Do not be afraid!" Peter said to Jesus, "If it is You, Lord, tell me to come to You on the water." Jesus said, "Come!" Peter got out of the boat and walked on the water to Jesus. But when he saw the strong wind, he was afraid. He began to go down in the water. He cried out, "Lord, save me!" At once Jesus put out His hand and took hold of him. Jesus said to Peter, "You have so little faith! Why did you doubt?"

MATTHEW 14:25–31 NLV

Close to My Heart

There are plenty of people in this world who say they are Christians, but many of them really don't know Me at all. Think about someone you know who says they know Me, but they don't really act like it. Will you commit to praying for that person? I'd like to show that person what a real friendship with Me can be—and you can help.

There's an old saying that says "actions speak louder than words." People can say a lot of things, but it's what's inside their hearts that really matters.

The Pharisees knew a lot about Old Testament laws. In fact, they prided themselves on looking good on the outside and strictly following all the laws. They thought they knew everything about Me, but their hearts were really quite far away.

Choosing to be My disciple doesn't mean you must follow all the rules and never mess up. Following Me means you have a real relationship with Me where you learn My Word and let My Spirit come alive in you. We discuss things. We're friends. You get to know My heart and My great love for you.

I invite you to come close to My heart and get to know the real Me. I want to bless our friendship and have conversations with you all day long. Our friendship will bring a lasting joy to your heart that bubbles up and blesses everyone around you.

"You hypocrites! Isaiah was right when he prophesied about you, for he wrote, 'These people honor me with their lips, but their hearts are far from me. Their worship is a farce, for they teach man-made ideas as commands from God.'" Then Jesus called to the crowd to come and hear. "Listen," he said, "and try to understand. It's not what goes into your mouth that defiles you; you are defiled by the words that come out of your mouth." Then the disciples came to him and asked, "Do you realize you offended the Pharisees by what you just said?" Jesus replied, "Every plant not planted by my heavenly Father will be uprooted, so ignore them. They are blind guides leading the blind, and if one blind person guides another, they will both fall into a ditch."

MATTHEW 15:7–14 NLT

Don't Be Afraid

I allowed some of My friends to go with Me on a mountain to witness something astonishing. My appearance changed into dazzling white light, and My face was as bright as the sun. Moses and Elijah appeared, and we started talking. Then My Father's voice was heard in the sky. My disciples were terrified after hearing My Father's voice booming from a cloud. They bowed down in fear with their faces to the ground. I knew they were scared, so I went to them. I put My hand on them and reminded them not to be afraid. They had nothing to fear in My presence—and neither do you, child.

I care about you more than you can imagine. And when you're with Me, you have no reason to be afraid. You can trust Me with your life. Want to know why? Because everything I do, I do out of love for you. I never lie, and I always keep My promises. I can turn any bad situation around and use it for good. Romans 8:28 (NIV) says, "We know that in all things God works for the good of those who love him, who have been called according to his purpose." Do you believe it?

That's why you don't have to be afraid when things seem a little scary. I am with you, and you can trust Me to care lovingly for you. Call on Me to help. I am always close.

Six days later Jesus took with Him Peter and James and his brother John. He led them up to a high mountain by themselves. He was changed in looks before them. His face was as bright as the sun. His clothes looked as white as light. Moses and Elijah were seen talking with Jesus. Then Peter said to Jesus, "Lord, it is good for us to be here. If You will let us, we will build three altars here. One will be for You and one for Moses and one for Elijah." While Peter was speaking, a bright cloud came over them. A voice from the cloud said, "This is My much-loved Son, I am very happy with Him. Listen to Him!" When the followers heard this, they got down on the ground on their faces and were very much afraid. Jesus came and put His hand on them. He said, "Get up! Do not be afraid."

MATTHEW 17:1–7 NLV

Beyond the Bubble

I know how easy it is to get caught up in your own world, dear one. Friends, family, school, church, sports. . . The list goes on! Those can all add great joy to your life—unless they become the bubble that you can't see beyond.

I want to help you keep your eyes on Me. I want to give you a bigger picture of your life—an eternal perspective. Let Me help you see beyond what's right in front of you. I don't want you to get stuck in a rut, where the opinions of your friends become the most important thing in your life. When that happens, those good relationships can become an idol. An idol is something that is more important to you than I am.

So let's talk about these things. Keep your eyes on Me, and I'll help you keep from making good things into idols, okay? I have kingdom work for you to do. And when you're more concerned about what your friends are thinking or doing, that will only get in the way of the work I want to accomplish in and through you.

There are some things you can do right now to help grow My kingdom right where you are. Talk to Me about ways you can serve in your church. I'll help you know which ministry is right for you. Think about going on a mission trip to another state or country. There are people all over the world who need to hear and experience My love.

So if you're serious about living this new resurrection life with Christ, act like it. Pursue the things over which Christ presides. Don't shuffle along, eyes to the ground, absorbed with the things right in front of you. Look up, and be alert to what is going on around Christ—that's where the action is. See things from his perspective. Your old life is dead. Your new life, which is your real life—even though invisible to spectators—is with Christ in God. He is your life. When Christ (your real life, remember) shows up again on this earth, you'll show up, too—the real you, the glorious you.

COLOSSIANS 3:1–4 MSG

Prayer and Accountability

Prayer is very powerful. Your prayers matter to Me, and they can accomplish a lot. Consider this: "Therefore, confess your sins to one another [your false steps, your offenses], and pray for one another, that you may be healed and restored. The heartfelt and persistent prayer of a righteous man (believer) can accomplish much [when put into action and made effective by God—it is dynamic and can have tremendous power]" (James 5:16 AMP).

I want you to come to Me and pray for others so that they can be healed and restored. I don't just mean physical bodies being healed and restored, but also hearts and minds being healed and made whole.

Confessing your sins to someone else and having them hold you accountable in faith and life goals is a great way to grow in maturity. Hebrews 10:24–25 (NIV) says, "And let us consider how we may spur one another on toward love and good deeds, not giving up meeting together, as some are in the habit of doing, but encouraging one another—and all the more as you see the Day approaching."

I want to help you find other believers who can help encourage you on the journey. Having some accountability partners to pray with and talk to can be a great joy in your life. Look for trustworthy and safe friends who love Me. Ask them if they're interested in getting together to pray. There's power when believers get together and talk to Me!

108

"I assure you and most solemnly say to you, whatever you bind [forbid, declare to be improper and unlawful] on earth shall have [already] been bound in heaven, and whatever you loose [permit, declare lawful] on earth shall have [already] been loosed in heaven. Again I say to you, that if two believers on earth agree [that is, are of one mind, in harmony] about anything that they ask [within the will of God], it will be done for them by My Father in heaven. For where two or three are gathered in My name [meeting together as My followers], I am there among them."

MATTHEW 18:18–20 AMP

Forgiveness and Reconciliation

When you sin, it breaks fellowship with Me. But when you come to Me to confess and repent, our relationship is quickly restored. I want you to quickly forgive others too. When you carry around unforgiveness in your heart, it gets very heavy and starts to cause all sorts of problems.

Think about who you might need to forgive. Let Me help. I can give you the strength to let things go. But let Me tell you something important: Forgiveness and reconciliation are not the same thing. Forgiveness is letting an offense go; reconciliation is restoring the relationship. Forgiveness is up to you; reconciliation takes two.

To restore a relationship, or to reconcile, it takes two people willing to repent and work out a problem *My way* so you can build trust for the future. If someone has severely wronged you, you are not required to trust that person again. But with My help, you can forgive them.

Forgiveness means you leave the judgment and punishment in My hands. You don't seek your own revenge. You let it go, knowing that I am just—and I see all sides of the story. I know exactly what happened. The person needing forgiveness will have to work at earning your trust if you are to reconcile in the future.

Come and talk to Me about this. I want to give you strength and the wisdom to know what to do next. I will lead you.

Do not let unwholesome [foul, profane, worthless, vulgar] words ever come out of your mouth, but only such speech as is good for building up others, according to the need and the occasion, so that it will be a blessing to those who hear [you speak]. And do not grieve the Holy Spirit of God [but seek to please Him], by whom you were sealed and marked [branded as God's own] for the day of redemption [the final deliverance from the consequences of sin]. Let all bitterness and wrath and anger and clamor [perpetual animosity, resentment, strife, fault-finding] and slander be put away from you, along with every kind of malice [all spitefulness, verbal abuse, malevolence]. Be kind and helpful to one another, tender-hearted [compassionate, understanding], forgiving one another [readily and freely], just as God in Christ also forgave you.
EPHESIANS 4:29–32 AMP

Blameless

Dear one, I want you to see yourself the way I do. Because of My work for you on the cross, you are holy and blameless in My sight. You can stand before Me without a single fault! Can you imagine this? Come right into My throne room and lift your head, daughter. The blood I shed for you on the cross covers all your sin and shame, now and forever. I love you. I want you close to Me.

I know everything about you, and I couldn't possibly love you any more or less than I already do. My love is unconditional. You don't have to earn it. There is no need to clean yourself up before you come to Me. Just come as you are. You are completely clean before Me because of what I've already done for you.

One of the enemy's goals is to attack your identity in Christ so that you won't know who you are or the power you have because of My Spirit living in you. Stand against any lies. Repent of believing anything but what I say about you. Tell Me when you're feeling less than worthy or ashamed. I want to speak truth and love over you. Come to Me when you feel like you're getting things all wrong. I will give you My perspective.

I want to empower you to believe and walk in the truth.

*For God in all his fullness was pleased to live in Christ,
and through him God reconciled everything to himself.
He made peace with everything in heaven and on earth
by means of Christ's blood on the cross. This includes you
who were once far away from God. You were his enemies,
separated from him by your evil thoughts and actions.
Yet now he has reconciled you to himself through the
death of Christ in his physical body. As a result, he has
brought you into his own presence, and you are holy and
blameless as you stand before him without a single fault.*
COLOSSIANS 1:19–22 NLT

Secure in My Arms

As My beloved daughter, you are held securely in My arms. The evil one cannot defeat you because of it. I want you to know, without a doubt, that you are secure in My love. Take a minute and imagine what this looks and feels like.

I am the one true God. There is no other. I've come to find you and free you from the punishment of sin and shame. I'm the only one who's made a way for you to have eternal life. I love you more than you could ever imagine, dear one. And I want you to share that love with others so they can know My abundant and eternal life too.

I want to give you power and courage to steer clear of anything that could take My place in your heart. I want to help you and give you warning signs when the enemy is up to his no-good schemes to discourage you, deceive you, and lead you away from Me. When you get that feeling in the pit of your stomach that something is wrong, pay attention to that! I created your body with a warning system for a reason. When that happens, remember to put on the armor I gave you and follow Me as I lead you back on the right path.

You are secure in My arms, daughter. Stay close to Me, and I will protect you from harm.

We know that God's children do not make a practice of sinning, for God's Son holds them securely, and the evil one cannot touch them. We know that we are children of God and that the world around us is under the control of the evil one. And we know that the Son of God has come, and he has given us understanding so that we can know the true God. And now we live in fellowship with the true God because we live in fellowship with his Son, Jesus Christ. He is the only true God, and he is eternal life. Dear children, keep away from anything that might take God's place in your hearts.

1 JOHN 5:18–21 NLT

A Love for My Word

The Pharisees and Sadducees, religious groups who were divided on interpretations of the scriptures, were often trying to trap Me in My words. I spoke plainly to them: "You are wrong because you do not know the Holy Writings or the power of God" (Matthew 22:29 NLV).

It's important to know what My Word has to say as you follow Me on this journey. One of the main ways that I speak to you is through My written word. I want you to know it and study it. Ask Me, and I'll help you develop a deep love for My Word.

The Bible is a powerful tool for My followers. Do you know that My Word is alive? My living Word can look inside your heart and help you know right from wrong with the help of the Holy Spirit.

In Psalm 119:11 (ESV), the psalmist wrote: "I have stored up your word in my heart, that I might not sin against you."

How can you hide My Word in your heart? First you need to read it. Make a habit of getting into My Word every day. Open your Bible and find a devotional like this one. Read the scriptures and try to memorize them whenever you can. My Spirit will help you learn My words and remember them when you need them!

Fall in love with My Word, dear one, and you will be blessed in many ways.

For the word of God is living and active and full of power [making it operative, energizing, and effective]. It is sharper than any two-edged sword, penetrating as far as the division of the soul and spirit [the completeness of a person], and of both joints and marrow [the deepest parts of our nature], exposing and judging the very thoughts and intentions of the heart. And not a creature exists that is concealed from His sight, but all things are open and exposed, and revealed to the eyes of Him with whom we have to give account. Inasmuch then as we [believers] have a great High Priest who has [already ascended and] passed through the heavens, Jesus the Son of God, let us hold fast our confession [of faith and cling tenaciously to our absolute trust in Him as Savior].

HEBREWS 4:12–14 AMP

117

What Should You Do with Your Life?

"What should I do with my life?" is the question I've heard so many young people get all worked up about. So many teens worry obsessively over these questions: What am I supposed to do with my life? Go to college? Get a job? Become a missionary? Some of My young friends are so afraid that they'll make the wrong choice, and so they remain stuck.

Let Me speak to this, child. I don't want you to obsess over the future. My mission is very simple, so please don't over-complicate it. Look here: "If I could speak all the languages of earth and of angels, but didn't love others, I would only be a noisy gong or a clanging cymbal. . . . If I understood all of God's secret plans. . .and if I had such faith that I could move mountains, but didn't love others, I would be nothing. If I gave everything I have to the poor. . .I could boast about it; but if I didn't love others, I would have gained nothing" (1 Corinthians 13:1–3 NLT).

What does this tell you? You could graduate with honors, become successful at many things, and achieve the American dream—but it would all count for nothing if you don't do it out of love for Me and love for others!

I gave you special gifts and talents that I want you to use to bless others as you make your mark on this world.

118

Develop them, and as you stay close to Me, I will lead you on the path that leads to life and love. Don't stress, My friend. We've got this. . .*together*.

The proud religious law-keepers got together when they heard that the religious group of people who believe no one will be raised from the dead were not able to talk anymore to Jesus. A proud religious law-keeper who knew the Law tried to trap Jesus. He said, "Teacher, which one is the greatest of the Laws?" Jesus said to him, "'You must love the Lord your God with all your heart and with all your soul and with all your mind.' This is the first and greatest of the Laws. The second is like it, 'You must love your neighbor as you love yourself.' All the Laws and the writings of the early preachers depend on these two most important Laws."
MATTHEW 22:34–40 NLV

Come to Me in Prayer

Spend some special time with Me today, dear one. I want to share My heart with you, and I want to hear yours. Remember, praying isn't about just submitting your wish list to Me like I'm some Santa Claus in the sky. I want a *real* relationship with you, where we both talk and listen. I want to spend time with you as My friend. I am real, and I want to have a moment-by-moment relationship with you.

I am your refuge—a place of safety and protection. Can you picture yourself being protected by Me? The Bible is full of imagery that you can take to heart. Read today's scripture and imagine the mountains crumbling and falling into the sea. How terrifying that might be for someone standing close by. But you don't have to be afraid, because I am with you. I am your refuge. Can you picture Me calming all your fears?

Exodus 14:14 (ESV) says: "The LORD will fight for you, and you have only to be silent." Be silent for a little while with Me. Allow Me to fill you with joy in My presence. Can you sense My love for you? Tell Me what's on your heart today. Talk to Me about what has you worried or fearful. I am here for you. Trust Me to fight your battles.

God is our refuge and strength, an ever-present help in trouble. Therefore we will not fear, though the earth give way and the mountains fall into the heart of the sea.... Come and see what the LORD has done, the desolations he has brought on the earth. He makes wars cease to the ends of the earth. He breaks the bow and shatters the spear; he burns the shields with fire. He says, "Be still, and know that I am God; I will be exalted among the nations, I will be exalted in the earth." The LORD Almighty is with us; the God of Jacob is our fortress.

PSALM 46:1–2, 8–11 NIV

Let Me Comfort You

Think about the last time you were really sad. Can you remember why you felt that way? Talk to Me about it. Bring Me anything that is making you sad or is heavy on your heart. I want to be a comfort to you.

Think about a mama duck with her babies or a mama hen with her little chicks all snuggled up under her wings. When a mama duck is heading toward water, her babies all follow her in a row. They know the voice of their mama and trust she'll lead them to safety.

Can you picture Me doing that for you, child? I created your imagination for a reason, and I use imagery in My Word to show how much I care for you. Go ahead and give it a try—imagine Me comforting you when you feel sad or lost.

Bring your sadness to Me. I am close to the brokenhearted, and I save those who are crushed in spirit (Psalm 34:18). I am closer than you think, dear one—as close as your next breath. When your heart is broken, I am with you. When your spirit feels crushed, I am close.

I hear your prayers, and My eyes are on you (Psalm 32:8). I see you. You are so important to Me, and I love you. Sit in My presence and allow Me to love and comfort you.

"O Jerusalem, Jerusalem, who murders the prophets and stones [to death] those [messengers] who are sent to her [by God]! How often I wanted to gather your children together [around Me], as a hen gathers her chicks under her wings, and you were unwilling. Listen carefully: your house is being left to you desolate [completely abandoned by God and destitute of His protection]! For I say to you, you will not see Me again [ministering to you publicly] until you say, 'Blessed [to be celebrated with praise] is He who comes in the name of the Lord!'"

MATTHEW 23:37–39 AMP

123

The Wrong Way

Be careful that no one leads you the wrong way. Many will stand up and claim to know Me. This is happening even in the church today. Some people say they have all the answers about Me, but they don't. Many of those people who claim to speak for Me are actually very far from Me.

But don't worry. I set My Spirit in your heart, and it's the Spirit's job to warn you when something is wrong. You just need to make sure you're paying attention. You'll have lots of teachers at church as you grow and mature as a young woman. Don't automatically believe everything someone tries to teach you about Me and My ways. If a teacher is leading you in a wrong way, remember this: My Spirit is alive inside you and will give you a warning signal. Something will just feel a little "off."

How will you know for sure if someone is teaching you something wrong? Get to know the truth from My Word so you can recognize when something is counterfeit. Whenever you get the "warning signal," grab your Bible and search My Word. Look up My answers. Ask Me to help you know what is right and wrong. I will instruct you and teach you the way you should go (Psalm 32:8).

You can count on Me to teach you the truth. Stay close to Me and hide My Word in your heart—and you won't be led astray.

Jesus answered, "Be careful that no one misleads you [deceiving you and leading you into error]. For many will come in My name [misusing it, and appropriating the strength of the name which belongs to Me], saying, 'I am the Christ (the Messiah, the Anointed),' and they will mislead many. You will continually hear of wars and rumors of wars. See that you are not frightened, for those things must take place, but that is not yet the end [of the age]. For nation will rise against nation, and kingdom against kingdom, and there will be famines and earthquakes in various places."

MATTHEW 24:4–7 AMP

The Parable of the Talents

When I was telling stories to My disciples and new friends, I often spoke in parables and picture stories. Many of the people I spoke to couldn't read, so I told them stories they could easily remember.

I once told a story that became known as the parable of the talents. (Back in Bible times, a "talent" was a large sum of money.) A landowner was going on a big trip, so he divided up his money and gave it to his servants according to their abilities. One servant was given five talents, another servant was given two talents, and the last one was given one talent. The man who was given five talents went right to work with the money and earned five more. The one who was given two talents earned two more. But the last servant was afraid that something bad would happen to his talent, so he buried it and didn't earn a thing. He did nothing for his master and got in trouble for it.

This parable has a double meaning. Can you think about what this means for your life? I have given each of My followers certain gifts and talents. I want you to use them to honor Me and bless others. How are you using the gifts I've given you? Let's talk about this—*together*. I want to teach you how to use your talents well.

"For the holy nation of heaven is like a man who was going to a country far away. He called together the servants he owned and gave them his money to use. He gave to one servant five pieces of money worth much. He gave to another servant two pieces of money worth much. He gave to another servant one piece of money worth much. He gave to each one as he was able to use it. Then he went on his trip. . . . The one who had received the five pieces of money worth much came and handed him five pieces more. He said, 'Sir, you gave me five pieces of money. See! I used it and made five more pieces.' His owner said to him, 'You have done well. You are a good and faithful servant. You have been faithful over a few things. I will put many things in your care. Come and share my joy.'"

MATTHEW 25:14–15, 20–21 NLV

Serving Me

My friend Paul wrote a letter to Timothy, telling him like it is! Check out what Paul said: "Tell those rich in this world's wealth to quit being so full of themselves and so obsessed with money, which is here today and gone tomorrow. Tell them to go after God, who piles on all the riches we could ever manage—to do good, to be rich in helping others, to be extravagantly generous. If they do that, they'll build a treasury that will last, gaining life that is truly life" (1 Timothy 6:17–19 MSG).

Sadly, having lots of money and getting more money is the number one priority on many people's lists. But I want something better for your life. I want you to seek after Me, not money and stuff that doesn't last. I want you to be rich in helping others.

Did you know that when you serve others you are really serving Me? Serving someone else means that you put that person's needs above your own; you find out what that person needs, and you do your best to help. "Truly I tell you, whatever you did for one of the least of these brothers and sisters of mine, you did for me" (Matthew 25:40 NIV).

When you see someone in need, picture Me being the one in need instead. Sit down with your family and think about ways you can get involved with needy people in your community. Find out how you can help, and remember you're serving Me as you do it!

"Then the King will say to those on His right side, 'Come, you who have been called by My Father. Come into the holy nation that has been made ready for you before the world was made. For I was hungry and you gave Me food to eat. I was thirsty and you gave Me water to drink. I was a stranger and you gave Me a room. I had no clothes and you gave Me clothes to wear. I was sick and you cared for Me. I was in prison and you came to see Me.' ... Then the King will say, 'For sure, I tell you, because you did it to one of the least of My brothers, you have done it to Me.'"

MATTHEW 25:34–36, 40 NLV

No Matter What Others Think

One day I was at My friend Simon's house when a woman named Mary came and poured expensive perfume on My head. This seemed very unusual to the rest of the people in the room! The disciples didn't understand what she was doing and thought that the cost of the perfume could've been better spent feeding the poor. But what Mary did for Me was special. It was a beautiful thing, and I told My disciples that. She was preparing Me for burial, something My disciples didn't understand yet.

Mary believed that she needed to give Me her expensive perfume and pour it on Me. Even if other people thought she was being strange or wasteful, she knew that what she was doing would honor Me. So Mary followed through, no matter what everyone else thought of her.

I know it can be hard to do some things I ask you to do. Sometimes it's difficult to worship Me when other people are around. You sometimes get embarrassed. But know this: I will defend you and take care of you as you carry out My plans for your life.

I promised that this special story of Mary would be told all throughout the world, and you're hearing it right now too. Be like Mary. You can be strong and confident in your faith, even when those around you may not understand what you're doing. I'm *with* you and *for* you, child.

Meanwhile, Jesus was in Bethany at the home of Simon, a man who had previously had leprosy. While he was eating, a woman came in with a beautiful alabaster jar of expensive perfume and poured it over his head. The disciples were indignant when they saw this. "What a waste!" they said. "It could have been sold for a high price and the money given to the poor." But Jesus, aware of this, replied, "Why criticize this woman for doing such a good thing to me? You will always have the poor among you, but you will not always have me. She has poured this perfume on me to prepare my body for burial. I tell you the truth, wherever the Good News is preached throughout the world, this woman's deed will be remembered and discussed."

MATTHEW 26:6–13 NLT

A Day of Rest

I gave you a good example to follow from the very beginning of time. After I created the world, I rested. Of course, I didn't have to. I *chose* to. I wanted My people to follow My example. I created a whole day of rest to help My people. I made you, so I know your body needs rest. Some adults who work in an office work five days a week and have the weekend free. Their bosses know that rest helps them be a better worker when they come back to the office on Monday.

Back in Bible times, My people would honor this day of rest in a special way. It was called "Shabbat," which is Hebrew for "Sabbath"—a word that means rest. In Jewish custom, the Sabbath begins at sunset on Friday and ends at sunset on Saturday. It's a full twenty-four hours of rest.

In American culture, the day of rest happened on Sunday. Stores would close and businesses would not open. But things are a bit different in your world right now. Everything is fast paced, and people are constantly working or using social media.

But, child, I have called you to be set apart—to be different. I want you to do things My way, a *better* way. It's hard to go against the flow of your world and take the time to rest. But it's important to Me that you slow down, focus on Me, and give your mind and body a good rest.

At that time Jesus walked through the grain-fields on the Day of Rest. As they went, His followers began to take some of the grain. The proud religious law-keepers said to Jesus, "See! Why are they doing what the Law says should not be done on the Day of Rest?" He said to them, "Have you not read what David did when he and his men were hungry? He went into the house of God when Abiathar was head religious leader of the Jews. He ate the special bread used in the religious worship. The Law says only the Jewish religious leaders may eat that. David gave some to those who were with him also." Jesus said to them, "The Day of Rest was made for the good of man. Man was not made for the Day of Rest. The Son of Man is Lord of the Day of Rest also."

MARK 2:23–28 NLV

Peace to You

I am known as the Prince of Peace, and I want to offer My peace to you. This is perfect peace—the kind that passes all understanding. Peace doesn't mean that everything is going great for you and working smoothly, free from any problems. No. It *does* mean that I am with you and giving you My perspective in the middle of *everything*.

I want you to let My peace rule in your heart. I can give you an inner calm as you walk with Me each day. When you focus your mind on Me, I will change your chaos to calm.

When you get in the daily habit of praying and giving all your problems, worries, and concerns to Me, it can help you avoid a lot of drama in your life! Drama might be entertaining on Netflix, but in real life it's messy and exhausting. It's not My will for you to stir up chaos or try to be the center of attention in every situation. Repent of that, and I will help you change those bad habits. I will give you wisdom as you center your heart on Me instead.

Bring Me all the unwanted drama and problems that are heavy on your heart today. Praise Me in worship. Turn on some of My favorite songs. Let Me exchange all the things that are weighing you down for My peace. I'll do it for you.

Let the peace of Christ [the inner calm of one who walks daily with Him] be the controlling factor in your hearts [deciding and settling questions that arise]. To this peace indeed you were called as members in one body [of believers]. And be thankful [to God always]. Let the [spoken] word of Christ have its home within you [dwelling in your heart and mind—permeating every aspect of your being] as you teach [spiritual things] and admonish and train one another with all wisdom, singing psalms and hymns and spiritual songs with thankfulness in your hearts to God. Whatever you do [no matter what it is] in word or deed, do everything in the name of the Lord Jesus [and in dependence on Him], giving thanks to God the Father through Him.

COLOSSIANS 3:15–17 AMP

Good Advice

We've talked about My friend Paul before. He wrote some letters to Timothy, a young minister, to encourage him not to give up. Paul gave some good advice that I want you to know too.

If you've invited Me into your life and chosen to follow Me, My Spirit is alive in you! The same Spirit lives in each of My followers—from children who've recently accepted Me to believers who've walked with Me for a lifetime. There is no "Holy Spirit Junior." It's Me—alive in you—that makes all the difference, no matter how old you are!

This is important: "Don't let anyone look down on you because you are young, but set an example for the believers in speech, in conduct, in love, in faith and in purity" (1 Timothy 4:12 NIV). I am the one who gives you the power to be an example to others—even older generations. You, as a teenager, can inspire and encourage young and old alike. I want to help you do this!

Many temptations and off-road adventures—things that aren't My will for you—are going to come your way as you continue to grow up. I want you to always pursue what is right. I will help you run away from situations that aren't pleasing to Me. Remember this verse: "He who is in you is greater than he who is in the world" (1 John 4:4 NKJV). With My power alive and at work in you, you have *nothing* to be afraid of.

Turn away from the sinful things young people want to do. Go after what is right. Have a desire for faith and love and peace. Do this with those who pray to God from a clean heart. Let me say it again. Have nothing to do with foolish talk and those who want to argue. It can only lead to trouble. A servant owned by God must not make trouble. He must be kind to everyone. He must be able to teach. He must be willing to suffer when hurt for doing good. Be gentle when you try to teach those who are against what you say. God may change their hearts so they will turn to the truth.

2 TIMOTHY 2:22–25 NLV

Mary and Martha

I went to visit My friends Mary and Martha one day. Martha was so excited to have Me visit her home that she went to work right away, getting the house ready and preparing for our visit. But her sister, Mary, chose to sit down at My feet and listen to what I had to say instead. Martha did what was expected of her. In those days, the women always served the men, preparing food and caring for their hospitality needs. But Mary went against the cultural norms to spend time with Me.

Martha realized what was happening, and she was upset that she was doing all the work herself! So she came to Me and pointed out that her sister wasn't helping. In love, I told Martha that Mary had made a better choice.

Sometimes people can get so distracted by the work they're doing *for* Me that they forget to take time to be *with* Me. That's what happened with Martha. She loved Me and was so happy to have Me in her home, but she got distracted by all the work.

Think about the things that distract you from Me. Make a commitment to come to Me in quiet, focused time every day so that we can talk. I'll help you get all the work done that I've called you to do, but you need to spend time with Me first. I'll help you know what is important and what's not.

As they went on their way, they came to a town where a woman named Martha lived. She cared for Jesus in her home. Martha had a sister named Mary. Mary sat at the feet of Jesus and listened to all He said. Martha was working hard getting the supper ready. She came to Jesus and said, "Do You see that my sister is not helping me? Tell her to help me." Jesus said to her, "Martha, Martha, you are worried and troubled about many things. Only a few things are important, even just one. Mary has chosen the good thing. It will not be taken away from her."

LUKE 10:38–42 NLV

A Habit of Prayer

I told My followers a story about a man's family, who were already in bed when a friend came and asked for a favor in the middle of the night. No one wants to get up in the middle of the night unless there's some sort of emergency, right? If you hear a knock on the door while you're in bed, you're likely to ignore it. But if that person *keeps* knocking, you're going to get up and see what they need, because there might be an emergency.

I want you to knock on the door of heaven. . .*persistently*. I want you to be faithful in your prayers. Keep coming to Me, and I will answer. Philippians 4:6–7 (NLT) is an important reminder: "Don't worry about anything; instead, pray about everything. Tell God what you need, and thank him for all he has done. Then you will experience God's peace, which exceeds anything we can understand. His peace will guard your hearts and minds as you live in Christ Jesus."

This is the habit I'd like you to get into: Don't worry. Pray about everything instead. Tell Me what you need. Thank Me for everything I have done and am doing in your life. That's how you experience My peace.

This is a promise to remember your whole life! When you get in the habit of praying instead of worrying, I will answer and fill you with peace.

Jesus said to them, "If one of you has a friend and goes to him in the night and says, 'Friend, give me three loaves of bread, for a friend of mine is on a trip and has stopped at my house. I have no food to give him.' The man inside the house will say, 'Do not trouble me. The door is shut. My children and I are in bed. I cannot get up and give you bread.' I say to you, he may not get up and give him bread because he is a friend. Yet, if he keeps on asking, he will get up and give him as much as he needs. I say to you, ask, and what you ask for will be given to you. Look, and what you are looking for you will find. Knock, and the door you are knocking on will be opened to you. For everyone who asks, will receive what he asks for. Everyone who looks, will find what he is looking for. Everyone who knocks, will have the door opened to him."

LUKE 11:5–10 NLV

141

Eternal Perspectives

Many people store up treasures on earth that have no meaning in heaven. Job 1:21 (AMP) says: "Naked (without possessions) I came [into this world] from my mother's womb, and naked I will return there. The LORD gave and the LORD has taken away; blessed be the name of the LORD."

It's important to remember that while you might work hard to earn money for "things," you can't take anything with you when you leave this world. I am your true inheritance.

And here's what I'm giving you instead: a new heaven and a new earth in restored bodies where there will be no tears, no pain (Revelation 21:4)—and you will reign with Me forever (Revelation 22:1–5)!

I want to give you an eternal perspective. I don't want you to hold on too tightly to "things." Everything you received on this earth is a gift. Hold it loosely and with thanksgiving. With an eternal perspective, you can also see problems and heartache in their proper light. Weeping may last for a little while, but joy will come (Psalm 30:5). So you don't have to be shaken when you get bad news. I am with you always.

Bring any sadness or heartache to Me. I want to help carry your load and help you see things through My eyes. I have eternal joy planned for you. Someday soon I will wipe every tear from all eyes and there will be no more death.

That's a promise you can count on!

LORD, you alone are my inheritance, my cup of blessing.
You guard all that is mine. The land you have given
me is a pleasant land. What a wonderful inheritance!
I will bless the LORD who guides me; even at night my
heart instructs me. I know the LORD is always with
me. I will not be shaken, for he is right beside me. No
wonder my heart is glad, and I rejoice. My body rests
in safety. For you will not leave my soul among the
dead or allow your holy one to rot in the grave. You will
show me the way of life, granting me the joy of your
presence and the pleasures of living with you forever.

PSALM 16:5–11 NLT

143

Totally Honest

You know, dear one, you can be totally honest with Me. You can't hide anything from Me. I already know how you feel about everything. I want to bring your thoughts and feelings to the surface so we can deal with them together. Stuffing them way down deep is not good for you.

My dear friend David wrote some brutal stuff in the book of Psalms. He gets very honest with Me. And I'm okay with that. I invite that. I want you to do the same. I am the safest place for you to share everything. I want to bring everything you're holding back out into the light. That way I can shine My light on all those thoughts and feelings and help you work them out.

I can change those heavy feelings of darkness and stress and sadness into joy and singing and thanksgiving! But it's a process. I deeply value you, and I am always careful with you. Just like a gentle shepherd carries his sheep back to the flock, I will care for you like that too.

When you allow Me to help you work through your issues and feelings, miraculous things start to happen. I know exactly what you need and how to get you from one step to the next. Will you trust Me with your deepest thoughts and feelings?

Cast all your cares, all your anxieties, all your worries, and all your concerns—once and for all—on Me. I care about you with deep affection, and I watch over you very carefully (1 Peter 5:7).

I pray to you, O LORD, my rock. Do not turn a deaf ear to me. For if you are silent, I might as well give up and die. Listen to my prayer for mercy as I cry out to you for help, as I lift my hands toward your holy sanctuary.... The LORD is my strength and shield. I trust him with all my heart. He helps me, and my heart is filled with joy. I burst out in songs of thanksgiving. The LORD gives his people strength. He is a safe fortress for his anointed king. Save your people! Bless Israel, your special possession. Lead them like a shepherd, and carry them in your arms forever.

PSALM 28:1–2; 7–9 NLT

The Prodigal

I once told a story about a father and his two sons. The younger son asked his father to give him his inheritance early. So he did . . .and the young man took it and left the country to waste his money on whatever he felt like. Pretty soon, he was out of food and completely broke. The young man had come to the lowest point of his life. He knew he had nothing left to do but go crawling back to his dad and beg forgiveness. He wasn't expecting to be treated like a son anymore, because he was ashamed of what he'd done and certain his father would be upset.

But the young man's father was watching and waiting for his son's return. The father was full of love and compassion for his son, and he ran out to meet him while he was still a long way off. His father celebrated the return of his lost son, forgiving him completely.

This is how I feel about you and about anyone who comes home to Me, dear one. This man became known as "the prodigal son." (A prodigal is a person who is reckless or wasteful. This can mean a person is wasteful with his money, foolish with his choices, or wastes his life.)

I want all prodigal children of Mine to come home to Me. Think about someone you know and love who is far from Me. Pray for that person.

And Jesus said, "There was a man who had two sons. The younger son said to his father, 'Father, let me have the part of the family riches that will be coming to me.' Then the father divided all that he owned between his two sons. Soon after that the younger son took all that had been given to him and went to another country far away. There he spent all he had on wild and foolish living. When all his money was spent, he was hungry. There was no food in the land. . . . 'I will get up and go to my father. I will say to him, "Father, I have sinned against heaven and against you. I am not good enough to be called your son. But may I be as one of the workmen you pay to work?"' The son got up and went to his father. While he was yet a long way off, his father saw him. The father was full of loving-pity for him. He ran and threw his arms around him and kissed him."

LUKE 15:11–14, 18–20 NLV

Strength from Me

I see you working hard, child. It's good to do your best work at school. It's good to work hard at improving the gifts and talents I've given you. The important thing to remember is that strength comes from Me! What are you currently working hard on? I have all the answers, and I'm very interested in helping you! Your math test? I can help you think clearly. Phys ed and sports? I am with you, helping you get stronger every day. Everything you're working on, call on Me for help and supernatural strength. Here's a great verse to memorize for times like these: "I can do all things through Christ who strengthens me" (Philippians 4:13 NKJV).

When you've met your goals, received that good grade, or nailed your latest challenge, remember Me then too. Let Me fill your heart with gratitude so that you can share your success with Me and thank Me for it.

As My Word promises, I am a safe place for you, and you can trust Me completely. Be thankful that I am a safe refuge for you. When you mess up *and* when you succeed, I am safe. I delight in you. I share your sorrows and your joys. Allow Me to be with you in those times.

Bring your successes and failures to Me now—and let Me love you through them. I am the solid rock under your feet. Everything you hope for comes from Me.

God, the one and only—I'll wait as long as he says.
Everything I hope for comes from him, so why not?
He's solid rock under my feet, breathing room for
my soul, an impregnable castle: I'm set for life. My
help and glory are in God—granite-strength and
safe-harbor-God—so trust him absolutely, people; lay
your lives on the line for him. God is a safe place to be.
. . . God said this once and for all; how many times have I
heard it repeated? "Strength comes straight from God."
PSALM 62:5–8, 11 MSG

My Kingdom

The Pharisees asked Me when the kingdom of God would come. They did not realize that through Me, the kingdom of God was already here. When you invite Me into your heart and choose to follow Me, the kingdom of God begins at that moment in your heart. My presence in your life *is* the kingdom of God. Your body is My temple. My kingdom on earth isn't a physical building or a church. It's alive inside you!

Yes, I am physically preparing a place for you in My Father's house. And one day soon I will come and take you to be with Me for all eternity. And there will be a day coming soon when I will make all things new and destroy all evil forever. But you don't have to wait for all that to happen to be a part of the kingdom of God. It's already begun!

Some people think you must endure this dark and crazy world and you won't be fully happy until heaven. But I want you to start living as part of My kingdom now. I want you to experience an abundant and joyful life (John 10:10) right here, no matter your circumstances. I want to fill you with peace, light, and love so that other people will want to know My kingdom of love too.

I want you to share these truths with the world, dear one! My kingdom is here.

Now having been asked by the Pharisees when the kingdom of God would come, He replied, "The kingdom of God is not coming with signs to be observed or with a visible display; nor will people say, 'Look! Here it is!' or, 'There it is!' For the kingdom of God is among you [because of My presence]." Then He said to the disciples, "The time will come when you will long to see [even] one of the days of the Son of Man, and you will not see it. They will say to you, 'Look [the Messiah is] there!' or 'Look [He is] here!' Do not go away [to see Him], and do not run after them. For just like the lightning, when it flashes out of one part of the sky, gives light to the other part of the sky, so [visible] will the Son of Man be in His day."

LUKE 17:20–24 AMP

Don't Give Up

I wanted My disciples to understand the importance of prayer and determination. So I told them another story. There was a widow who kept going to see a judge about a matter that was very important to her. She was looking for the judge to right a wrong that had been done to her. The judge didn't care about God or people, so he sent her away. But she kept coming back until the judge was sick of seeing her! He finally did what she asked because he wanted her to quit bothering him. If a wicked judge will grant a request due to someone's persistence, wouldn't a God *who actually loves you* grant your requests even more? Yes! I love you, dear one. I don't ever get annoyed by your prayers.

First Thessalonians 5:16–18 (ESV) says: "Rejoice always, pray without ceasing, give thanks in all circumstances; for this is the will of God in Christ Jesus for you."

I want you to keep coming to Me about everything. I want to help you sort things out. If something is outside My plan and purpose for your life, I will let you know. The important thing is to bring your thoughts, plans, and feelings to Me first. Come to Me in prayer and praise, always. This is My will for you!

Many people go through life searching aimlessly for what to do, but I've made it so simple: rejoice, give thanks in every circumstance, and pray!

Pray always, and don't give up, My friend!

One day Jesus told his disciples a story to show that they should always pray and never give up. "There was a judge in a certain city," he said, "who neither feared God nor cared about people. A widow of that city came to him repeatedly, saying, 'Give me justice in this dispute with my enemy.' The judge ignored her for a while, but finally he said to himself, 'I don't fear God or care about people, but this woman is driving me crazy. I'm going to see that she gets justice, because she is wearing me out with her constant requests!'"

LUKE 18:1–5 NLT

A Sacrifice

I was in the temple courts teaching one day, and I saw people giving their gifts to the temple treasury. Rich people were putting in their gifts, and then I saw a poor widow put in two small coins. "Truly I say to you, this poor widow has put in [proportionally] more than all of them; for they all put in gifts from their abundance; but she out of her poverty put in all she had to live on" (Luke 21:3–4 AMP).

Even though the rich men put in a bigger amount, the poor woman had given more. How? . . . Because she gave *everything* she had, trusting that God would take care of her. The rich men put in a lot, but it was money they didn't even need. It didn't cost them much of anything to give their money. The poor woman gave sacrificially. This means that she gave up something of great value to her as an act of worship to God.

What would it be like to worship Me sacrificially like that? Quiet your mind for a moment, and think about this. Is there something you can give of your time, talents, or treasure that would be a sacrifice for you? (A sacrifice is giving up something that costs you something, not just money. When something is a sacrifice, it means it isn't an easy thing to do.)

Discuss the idea of sacrifice with your family. How can you sacrifice something of yourselves to worship Me? Can you sacrifice something to bless others that are less fortunate than you?

Now [remember] this: he who sows sparingly will also reap sparingly, and he who sows generously [that blessings may come to others] will also reap generously [and be blessed]. Let each one give [thoughtfully and with purpose] just as he has decided in his heart, not grudgingly or under compulsion, for God loves a cheerful giver [and delights in the one whose heart is in his gift]. And God is able to make all grace [every favor and earthly blessing] come in abundance to you, so that you may always [under all circumstances, regardless of the need] have complete sufficiency in everything [being completely self-sufficient in Him], and have an abundance for every good work and act of charity.

2 CORINTHIANS 9:6–8 AMP

Tell My Story

People want to know that a friendship with Me can make a difference in their lives. Has it made a difference for you? I would like you to take some time and write down all the ways you've seen Me work in your life. This is called a testimony. Your testimony is very important. It tells of how you met Me and the difference I've made in your life. Think about all the prayers that I've answered for you since we've become friends. Go back to the very beginning. Ask your parents to help you remember when you first accepted Me into your heart. That's the beginning of our adventure together. When have I answered your prayers in miraculous ways? When have I given you peace in a hard situation? When have I helped you when you needed it most? . . .

I told My disciples to tell everyone about everything they saw and heard from Me. My disciples shared their stories of how I changed their lives, and My message kept on spreading throughout all of history. My followers have never stopped sharing the truth about My love, and that's why you know about it today. I want you to continue this life-changing practice with the people around you too.

Pray for open doors to share My love with others. I will give you the courage to share your story about Me with the people in your life who need to hear it.

Jesus said to them, "These are the things I told you while I was yet with you. All things written about Me in the Law of Moses and in the Books of the early preachers and in the Psalms must happen as they said they would happen." Then He opened their minds to understand the Holy Writings. He said to them, "It is written that Christ should suffer and be raised from the dead after three days. It must be preached that men must be sorry for their sins and turn from them. Then they will be forgiven. This must be preached in His name to all nations beginning in Jerusalem. You are to tell what you have seen."

LUKE 24:44–48 NLV

Good Things Are Coming

Remember Jeremiah 29:11? Make sure that verse is highlighted in your Bible. Write it down and hang it on your wall. I know the plans I have for you! This verse is a reminder from Me that I have good things in store for you. Right before I went back to heaven, I prayed this over My followers. I prayed that good would come to them. I want that for you too, child. I want you to find Me and know Me personally. I want you to believe and trust that you are never alone—and that you have full access to the greatest power alive. What good news!

Psalm 31:19 (GNT) says: "How wonderful are the good things you keep for those who honor you! Everyone knows how good you are, how securely you protect those who trust you." Be thankful for this, My friend. I am a good and loving God. Following Me is the most important decision you can ever make. I will fill your life with adventure and love and peace. . .if you let Me.

This doesn't mean life on earth won't have problems. It will. Troubles will come. But what good adventure doesn't have a bit of danger in it? Would you want to read a book or watch a movie that didn't have some sort of trouble to overcome? Here's the thing: I promise to be with you always—even in the midst of trouble—and I will give you a special kind of peace that goes beyond your understanding (Philippians 4:7).

"See! I will send you what My Father promised. But you are to stay in Jerusalem until you have received power from above." Jesus led them out as far as Bethany. Then He lifted up His hands and prayed that good would come to them. And while He was praying that good would come to them, He went from them (*and was taken up to heaven and they worshiped Him). Then they went back to Jerusalem with great joy. They spent all their time in the house of God honoring and giving thanks to God.

LUKE 24:49–53 NLV

The Good News

If there is one verse in the Bible that you decide to memorize, John 3:16 should be the priority. Take some time right now to write it down. Take the time to memorize it: "For God so loved the world that he gave his one and only Son, that whoever believes in him shall not perish but have eternal life" (NIV).

This famous verse sums up the entire gospel. It's the good news! It's also a great verse to know by heart so that you can share it with people who want to know more about Me.

John 3:17 is very important too. I came not to condemn you but to save you. I am the Savior of the world. When you call on My name and put your trust in Me, you are guaranteed a life that lasts forever—with Me in eternity. When you make Me the Lord of your life, it means you are choosing to let Me lead you all the days of your life. I will put a desire in your heart to follow My Word and My ways.

Now let's think about your friends and family who don't know Me. Will you write their names down? Pray for them daily. I want to give you courage to share the good news with them at just the right time. I am the one who calls people to Myself, and I can use your prayers and your testimony to open their hearts to the truth.

For God so loved the world that he gave his one and only Son, that whoever believes in him shall not perish but have eternal life. For God did not send his Son into the world to condemn the world, but to save the world through him. Whoever believes in him is not condemned, but whoever does not believe stands condemned already because they have not believed in the name of God's one and only Son. This is the verdict: Light has come into the world, but people loved darkness instead of light because their deeds were evil. Everyone who does evil hates the light, and will not come into the light for fear that their deeds will be exposed. But whoever lives by the truth comes into the light, so that it may be seen plainly that what they have done has been done in the sight of God.

JOHN 3:16–21 NIV

Filled to the Brim

I was traveling through Samaria one day, and I sat down by a well to take a rest. A Samaritan woman came to get water. Samaritans were a hated group of people. Jewish people would have refused to speak to them, especially to a woman.

But I came for *all* people. I cherish the people I created. Women and children are very special to Me. Society wasn't like that back in those days. Women and children were often treated poorly or used and abused. This grieves My heart.

I had a good conversation with the Samaritan woman. She lived a sinful life and needed to hear about My offer of everlasting life. I wanted her to know the source of My living water so she wouldn't have to keep going back to abusive relationships that could never fill her with the love she needed.

Isaiah 58:11 (ICB) says: "The Lord will always lead you. He will satisfy your needs in dry lands. He will give strength to your bones. You will be like a garden that has much water. You will be like a spring that never runs dry."

Just like I told the Samaritan woman, I can fill *you* up with living water that brings life to everything—and everyone— around! I can fill you to the brim with love that will spill out and bless others. Just come to Me, and let Me do it!

When a Samaritan woman came to draw water, Jesus said to her, "Will you give me a drink?" (His disciples had gone into the town to buy food.) The Samaritan woman said to him, "You are a Jew and I am a Samaritan woman. How can you ask me for a drink?" (For Jews do not associate with Samaritans.) Jesus answered her, "If you knew the gift of God and who it is that asks you for a drink, you would have asked him and he would have given you living water." . . . Jesus answered, "Everyone who drinks this water will be thirsty again, but whoever drinks the water I give them will never thirst. Indeed, the water I give them will become in them a spring of water welling up to eternal life."

JOHN 4:7–10, 13–14 NIV

My Power

I am the one who stretched out the heavens and brings out the wind from My storehouse. My power is beyond anything you can imagine. And yet, My heart is set on you, dear one. I love and care about you more than anything else in all My creation. Come to Me and pray. Tell Me what you think. I love to hear you praise and worship Me. I love to hear your voice.

Now look at your problems. Do they still seem big to you? Trust Me. Bring Me the issues that weigh heavily on your heart today. Think of My raw power. Am I powerful enough to help you through whatever you have going on? Do I really care about you enough to help? The answer to both of those questions is *yes*!

I am the God who speaks water into existence with the sound of My voice. The wind and the waves obey Me because I created them. I can take care of anything you are facing. I am the one true God—the God of truth. I don't want you to run to people and things for help. Distractions that you welcome into your life to help you feel better about yourself can turn into idols that take your attention off Me. Bring Me your worries and your frustrations. Come to Me with your problems, and let Me give My perspective.

But the LORD is the true God and the God who is Truth; He is the living God and the everlasting King. The earth quakes and shudders at His wrath, and the nations are not able to endure His indignation. . . . God made the earth by His power; He established the world by His wisdom and by His understanding and skill He has stretched out the heavens. When He utters His voice, there is a tumult of waters in the heavens, and He causes the clouds and the mist to ascend from the end of the earth; He makes lightning for the rain, and brings out the wind from His treasuries and from His storehouses.

JEREMIAH 10:10, 12–13 AMP

Teenage Girls

Being a teenage girl can be hard—I know it! Young women are designed with a desire to be cherished and valued. When they don't come to Me to fill that hole, they look to be filled up in other destructive ways. Many girls who don't know who they really are end up making very poor choices to temporarily feel better about themselves. The truth is these girls are empty and acting out of an orphan spirit.

Try to remember that the next time you encounter some "mean girls." Pray for them, and then go on about your life. I don't want you to worry about what others are saying about you. And I certainly don't want you trying to fit in with girls like that. When My power is at work in you, you can be confident in who you are as My child, no matter what anyone else thinks.

Rumors and lies hurt. But as you bring them to Me, I'll replace them with My truth. You are a dearly loved daughter of the King of kings! You have access to all My riches and knowledge. You can go boldly before My throne because of how loved you are. What truth do you need to be reminded of today? Let Me speak to your heart.

Being confident in who you are—*in Me*—comes from spending time in My Word and in prayer. I want you to be yourself—the wonderfully amazing girl I created! I am with you.

We faithfully preach the truth. God's power is working in us. We use the weapons of righteousness in the right hand for attack and the left hand for defense. We serve God whether people honor us or despise us, whether they slander us or praise us. We are honest, but they call us impostors. We are ignored, even though we are well known. We live close to death, but we are still alive. We have been beaten, but we have not been killed. Our hearts ache, but we always have joy. We are poor, but we give spiritual riches to others. We own nothing, and yet we have everything.

2 CORINTHIANS 6:7–10 NLT

Tough Decisions

I had some followers early on who didn't fully trust Me. They turned away from Me and stopped following. They thought a life of faith was too difficult. Some of My truths can be offensive and difficult at times—especially if I'm saying something you really don't want to hear!

You're going to have to make a lot of important choices as you grow up. Will you stay strong in your faith? What will you do with your life? Will you give in to pressure from friends and make choices you know are wrong? Growing up and making decisions can be a scary thing. But remember, I am with you.

You have My Spirit alive and at work inside you to help you make important decisions. You can be sure that I will lead you if you're listening for My voice. Isaiah 30:21 (ICB) says, "If you go the wrong way—to the right or to the left—you will hear a voice behind you. It will say, 'This is the right way. You should go this way.'"

This may not be a voice you hear out loud (but if I want to speak to you out loud, I surely will!); it's often like a warning system inside your head and your heart. Remember, I want you to know My voice. I will make things clear to you if you seek Me.

"The Spirit gives life; the flesh counts for nothing. The words I have spoken to you—they are full of the Spirit and life. Yet there are some of you who do not believe." For Jesus had known from the beginning which of them did not believe and who would betray him. He went on to say, "This is why I told you that no one can come to me unless the Father has enabled them." From this time many of his disciples turned back and no longer followed him.

"You do not want to leave too, do you?" Jesus asked the Twelve. Simon Peter answered him, "Lord, to whom shall we go? You have the words of eternal life. We have come to believe and to know that you are the Holy One of God."

JOHN 6:63–69 NIV

Living Water and Fruit

"Rivers of living water will flow from the heart of the one who puts his trust in Me" (John 7:38 NLV). Isn't it cool to think that you have My living water flowing through you? What do you think I might like you to do with all that water? Take a minute to think about that. Can you picture My living water flowing through you right now? Psalm 1:3 (NIV) says: "That person is like a tree planted by streams of water, which yields its fruit in season and whose leaf does not wither—whatever they do prospers." Now picture a tree planted by a stream. Does it look healthy? Why?

When you live your life for Me and allow Me to fill you with My living water, you become like a healthy tree—a tree that produces a lot of fruit—planted right by a stream. Trees that produce a lot of fruit can feed and bring joy to a lot of people. And so can you, child!

As you grow in your faith and learn to depend on Me, I will fill you with more and more living water to produce more and more fruit. The fruits of the Spirit are what I'm talking about. These fruits are love, joy, peace, patience, kindness, goodness, faithfulness, gentleness, and self-control (Galatians 5:22–23). What fruit do you need to grow more of? Talk to Me about this. We may have some weeding and watering to do!

Now on the last and most important day of the feast, Jesus stood and called out [in a loud voice], "If anyone is thirsty, let him come to Me and drink! He who believes in Me [who adheres to, trusts in, and relies on Me], as the Scripture has said, 'From his innermost being will flow continually rivers of living water.'" But He was speaking of the [Holy] Spirit, whom those who believed in Him [as Savior] were to receive afterward. The Spirit had not yet been given, because Jesus was not yet glorified (raised to honor).

JOHN 7:37–39 AMP

A Light in the Dark

I know things look very dark in the world. People are always fighting with each other. Some countries hate other countries, and they start wars. Too many people spend more time with their face in a screen than they do living real life. The enemy loves to keep people distracted and busy. When evil gets ahold of a person, they make some super bad choices.

That's why My light is so important in your world. And, child, you have it!

I gave you My light so that you never have to walk in darkness. You don't ever have to follow the crowd into dark places. You can be a leader with a bright light—a leader people will want to follow. Think about a very dark room when all the electricity goes out. All you need is one small candle to bring some light into the darkness. I can do great things with the light I've placed inside you.

When people see a light in the darkness, they want it. They're drawn to it. They'll want to know what causes you to be joyful and loving. They'll want to know where that light and love come from. I want you to shine your light as bright as possible! You do that by being yourself! You do that by letting My light and love flow out of you. You can be a bright leader in a distracted, dark world.

This is the message we have heard from him and declare to you: God is light; in him there is no darkness at all. If we claim to have fellowship with him and yet walk in the darkness, we lie and do not live out the truth. But if we walk in the light, as he is in the light, we have fellowship with one another, and the blood of Jesus, his Son, purifies us from all sin. If we claim to be without sin, we deceive ourselves and the truth is not in us. If we confess our sins, he is faithful and just and will forgive us our sins and purify us from all unrighteousness.

1 JOHN 1:5–9 NIV

The Enemy

Let's talk about our enemy today, dear one. It's important that you know what he's up to so that you can be prepared. I will tell you the truth, and I will give you hope. I don't want you to be afraid.

It's true that you have an enemy who is out to kill, steal, and destroy you (John 10:10). I know that sounds scary. But here's the truth: My power is ultimate, and the power of My enemy doesn't even come close.

Satan is a defeated foe. A lame duck. He is a liar, so he will try to get you to believe that he is more powerful than he really is. Tell him the truth—this will cause him to slink away.

Here's what you need to know about the enemy:

- *Satan is real (1 Peter 5:8).*

- *He is a liar (John 8:44) and sometimes pretends to be good (2 Corinthians 11:14).*

- *He'll try to lead you away from Me (2 Corinthians 11:3).*

- *He's defeated (1 John 3:8).*

- *My power is so much greater than the enemy's (1 John 4:4).*

- *I protect you with My armor (Ephesians 6:10–18).*

- *You are safe from the devil when you trust in Me (James 4:7).*

When you're scared because you're facing something that comes from the enemy, call out to Me. Let Me handle it. Say My name! Don't focus on your fears—focus on Me. You are safe.

Jesus said to them, "If God were your father, you would love Me. I came from God. I did not come on My own, but God sent Me. Why do you not understand what I say? It is because you do not want to hear My teaching. The devil is your father. You are from him. You want to do the sinful things your father, the devil, wants you to do. He has been a killer from the beginning. The devil has nothing to do with the truth. There is no truth in him. It is expected of the devil to lie, for he is a liar and the father of lies. I tell you the truth and that is why you do not put your trust in Me. Which one of you can say I am guilty of sin? If I tell you the truth, why do you not believe Me? Whoever is born of God listens to God's Word. You do not hear His Word because you are not born of God."
JOHN 8:42–47 NLV

Trust Me with Everything

I've mentioned My friends Mary and Martha to you before. They had a brother named Lazarus. I loved their family. Well, a time came when Lazarus got very sick. Mary and Martha tried to take good care of him, but he kept getting sicker and sicker. They sent for Me to come. But I didn't go to them right away. There was a reason for that: I wanted them to learn to trust Me.

I waited a few more days, and then I went to see them. But while I was traveling there, Lazarus died. Martha was upset at Me for not coming right away. But she didn't really know how powerful I was yet, even though she was My friend. She didn't understand that I have all power over life and death. Mary was upset too.

I had compassion for them and cried right along with them. I went to the tomb where Lazarus was buried. Martha was worried about the smell and didn't want Me to go into the tomb. But I had the stone rolled away and said, "Lazarus, come out!" (John 11:43). So, of course, he did just that! I brought him back to life. This was My plan. My friends needed to know that I was all-powerful and trustworthy. Many people saw My glory that day, and they put their faith in Me.

What I've done before, I can do again. Trust Me, friend. You can trust Me with *everything*!

So they took away the stone. Then Jesus looked up and said, "Father, I thank you that you have heard me. I knew that you always hear me, but I said this for the benefit of the people standing here, that they may believe that you sent me." When he had said this, Jesus called in a loud voice, "Lazarus, come out!" The dead man came out, his hands and feet wrapped with strips of linen, and a cloth around his face. Jesus said to them, "Take off the grave clothes and let him go." Therefore many of the Jews who had come to visit Mary, and had seen what Jesus did, believed in him.

JOHN 11:41–45 NIV

Spending Time with Me

I want you to know something, daughter. The time you spend with Me will accomplish more than anything else you could ever do. There is no one else who can do what I can do.

Jeremiah 32:17 (ESV) says: "Ah, Lord GOD! It is you who have made the heavens and the earth by your great power and by your outstretched arm! Nothing is too hard for you." Do you believe it? It's true. Nothing is too hard for Me. I am bigger than anything you're facing. I'm stronger than your biggest fear. I want to fill your heart with peace as you learn to trust Me and come to Me with your worries and cares.

Come to Me so I can teach you My ways. I will give you My strength to follow My will for your life. You don't have to muster up all the strength on your own to do all that I've called you to do. That would exhaust you, dear one. My power is alive and at work in you. I am the one who gives you strength.

Continue bringing everything on your heart to Me. Lay it down. Surrender your plans to Me. Let Me fill you with My love, power, and blessing. I won't weigh you down with worries. I will give you peace and strength to make it through the day. Spending time with Me will make all the difference in your day-to-day life.

*O Lord, you are so good, so ready to forgive, so full of
unfailing love for all who ask for your help. Listen closely
to my prayer, O LORD; hear my urgent cry. I will call to
you whenever I'm in trouble, and you will answer me.
No pagan god is like you, O Lord. None can do what
you do! All the nations you made will come and bow
before you, Lord; they will praise your holy name.
For you are great and perform wonderful deeds. You
alone are God. Teach me your ways, O LORD, that I may
live according to your truth! Grant me purity of heart, so
that I may honor you. With all my heart I will praise you,
O Lord my God. I will give glory to your name forever,
for your love for me is very great. You have
rescued me from the depths of death.*

PSALM 86:5–13 NLT

Loving Others

I gave My disciples a new command: love each other. Loving each other wasn't a new law. I told the Hebrew people in the Old Testament to love each other too. But loving others *like I do* was new. No one had ever loved them like I did. I laid down My life for each of them; and I do the same for you too.

I want you to start seeing other people through My eyes. I want you to bring Me the difficult people and ask Me for help to love them well. I can give you new insights. I can help you see the broken spirit that lives inside each difficult person. I can help you love them, despite their failures and flaws.

People will know that you follow Me by how well you love. I made each person in My image, and I want everyone to find the freedom from sin that their hearts long for. I want the world to know My love. And, child, you have a special part in that!

Can you try treating everyone you meet like they were Me? And loving them like they were Me? What would it be like to treat your brother and sister like they were Me instead of treating them like annoying family members who sometimes get on your nerves? Do you think that would change your family? You bet it would! Why not give it a try?

You can start changing the world *today* by loving people the way I want you to.

When he was gone, Jesus said, "Now the Son of Man is glorified and God is glorified in him. If God is glorified in him, God will glorify the Son in himself, and will glorify him at once. My children, I will be with you only a little longer. You will look for me, and just as I told the Jews, so I tell you now: Where I am going, you cannot come. A new command I give you: Love one another. As I have loved you, so you must love one another. By this everyone will know that you are my disciples, if you love one another."
JOHN 13:31–35 NIV

Trouble and Deep Water

"Do not let your heart be troubled. You have put your trust in God, put your trust in Me also" (John 14:1 NLV). This is a great verse to bring to mind when you are scared or worried. I want you to trust Me and not be afraid. Be still and know that I'm God (Psalm 46:10). I am good, and I love you so very much.

Here is a truth I want you to know, dear one: "He reached down from heaven and rescued me; he drew me out of deep waters. He rescued me from my powerful enemies, from those who hated me and were too strong for me. They attacked me at a moment when I was in distress, but the LORD supported me. He led me to a place of safety; he rescued me because he delights in me" (Psalm 18:16–19 NLT).

"Deep water" in this verse means more than just rescuing you from a lake or an ocean. Deep water can also mean any hard times that you are having at school, in your family, or with your friends. Think about the last time you were in deep water. How did you feel?

I care about all of it—and I want to reach down from heaven and support you. My Word reminds you that I will lead you to a place of safety. I can bring the people and supplies to meet any need you have. Just talk to Me about it. Let Me show you what I can do.

182

I love You, O Lord, my strength. The Lord is my rock, and my safe place, and the One Who takes me out of trouble. My God is my rock, in Whom I am safe. He is my safe-covering, my saving strength, and my strong tower. I call to the Lord, Who has the right to be praised. And I am saved from those who hate me. . . . He sent from above, and took me. He lifted me out of many waters. He took me away from the powerful one who fights against me, and from those who hated me. They were too strong for me. They stood against me in the day of my trouble. But the Lord was my strength. He brought me out into a big place. He gave me a safe place, because He was pleased with me.

PSALM 18:1–3, 16–19 NLV

Fully Known, Fully Loved

My friend Moses was reluctant to lead. I had to be very clear with him about what I needed him to do. And I gave him courage and strength to do the work I called him to.

No matter where you are or what kind of personality you have, I am calling *you* to be a leader too. Even if you are quiet and shy, I can use you to lead with a gentle strength in many situations. If you are outgoing and extroverted, I can use your spirit of enthusiasm to share My love with many. The point is to allow Me to use the personality I've given you in the way that I see fit.

Just like I knew Moses' name, I know yours; in fact, I know everything about you. I put you on earth at this exact time in history, and in the exact place you live, for a purpose (Acts 17:26). I want you to know Me. I want you to learn to love Me and to love others through Me. I want you to truly believe that My presence will be with you wherever you go!

I want to teach you My ways, dear one. I will help you become the leader I've created you to be. I gave you a unique personality on purpose. There's no one else in the whole world who's exactly like you.

Will you sit in My presence today and just let Me love you? Sometimes that's the only thing that's needed. You are fully known and fully loved, child.

184

Moses said to the LORD, "You have been telling me, 'Lead these people,' but you have not let me know whom you will send with me. You have said, 'I know you by name and you have found favor with me.' If you are pleased with me, teach me your ways so I may know you and continue to find favor with you. Remember that this nation is your people." The LORD replied, "My Presence will go with you, and I will give you rest." Then Moses said to him, "If your Presence does not go with us, do not send us up from here. How will anyone know that you are pleased with me and with your people unless you go with us? What else will distinguish me and your people from all the other people on the face of the earth?" And the LORD said to Moses, "I will do the very thing you have asked, because I am pleased with you and I know you by name."

EXODUS 33:12–17 NIV

Peace beyond Your Understanding

Think about a peaceful place. What does it look like? Maybe near an ocean with a light breeze? Maybe a grassy field covered in butterflies? Peaceful places can be great for relaxation. But having peace in your heart doesn't mean that everything is perfect and nothing is going wrong in your life. That's not *real* peace.

I am the one who gives true peace. When you experience the true peace that only I can give, you experience a deep knowing, that no matter what happens to you or what is going wrong in your life. . .I am still in control. This type of peace is the peace that goes beyond what your human mind can understand; it doesn't make sense sometimes. How can people have peace when chaos is happening all around them? It's My supernatural peace that is evident in times like this—an inner calm, despite your circumstances.

Today's verse says something very important that I want you to remember: I don't give gifts like the world does. When you receive something from someone on earth, those gifts usually don't last for very long. They wear out. But My gift of peace is eternal and available to anyone who calls on Me as their Savior. This means that you don't have to be afraid, no matter what is happening in your life. Your heart can rest as you trust Me to take care of you.

"Peace I leave with you; My [perfect] peace I give to you; not as the world gives do I give to you. Do not let your heart be troubled, nor let it be afraid. [Let My perfect peace calm you in every circumstance and give you courage and strength for every challenge.] You heard Me tell you, 'I am going away, and I am coming back to you.' If you [really] loved Me, you would have rejoiced, because I am going [back] to the Father, for the Father is greater than I. I have told you now before it happens, so that when it does take place, you may believe and have faith [in Me]."

JOHN 14:27–29 AMP

Grapes on the Vine

You know I loved telling stories that My followers could always remember. Many of them were farmers, and lots of them couldn't read. My stories were easy to remember and taught My friends special things about My kingdom.

One day I told them about grapes. They all knew plenty about that fruit. I told them that I was the vine and they were the branches. If a branch is cut off, it can't live; it won't bear any fruit.

The next time you have grapes in your refrigerator, take them out and look at them. How many grapes are still attached to the vine? Those are the firm, fresh grapes. Do you see any that have fallen off the vine in the bottom of the package or container? They are usually squishy and gross. You usually throw those away.

This tells us a lot about your relationship with Me. When you are walking close to Me—by talking to Me, worshipping Me, and reading My Word—you are attached to the vine. Your heart is full of Me, and you are fresh and inviting. But when you fall away from the vine, you can become grumpy and selfish, just like a grape that's squishy and gross.

What kind of fruit do you want to be? Squishy or fresh? Stay close to Me, and I will give you abundant life that bears much fruit. Apart from Me, you can do nothing.

"I am the true Vine. My Father is the One Who cares for the Vine. He takes away any branch in Me that does not give fruit. Any branch that gives fruit, He cuts it back so it will give more fruit. You are made clean by the words I have spoken to you. Get your life from Me and I will live in you. No branch can give fruit by itself. It has to get life from the vine. You are able to give fruit only when you have life from Me. I am the Vine and you are the branches. Get your life from Me. Then I will live in you and you will give much fruit. You can do nothing without Me."

JOHN 15:1–5 NLV

Stay in My Love

In John 15, I told My followers how they can show their love for Me—by obeying My commands. Do you know what My two most important commands are? I made them simple so you wouldn't forget. My commands are to love God *and* love others. Everything else depends on those two things (Matthew 22:36–40).

Three things will last forever—faith, hope, and love—and the greatest of these is love (1 Corinthians 13:13). My friend Paul wrote the book of 1 Corinthians as I inspired him to. It is a reminder that nothing matters if it isn't done with love.

Do you remember when you first felt My love? How did you feel? What did you do? Remember the time when you first asked Me to come into your heart and be the Lord of your life. Think about what that was like. Write down anything you can remember.

I don't want you to forget your first love, dear one. Revelation 2:4–5 (ICB) says: "You have left the love you had in the beginning. So remember where you were before you fell. Change your hearts and do what you did at first."

Jude 1:21 (NIV) says, "Keep yourselves in God's love as you wait for the mercy of our Lord Jesus Christ to bring you to eternal life."

Staying in My love means seeking Me first and talking to Me about *everything*.

"I have loved you just as the Father has loved Me; remain in My love [and do not doubt My love for you]. If you keep My commandments and obey My teaching, you will remain in My love, just as I have kept My Father's commandments and remain in His love. I have told you these things so that My joy and delight may be in you, and that your joy may be made full and complete and overflowing. This is My commandment, that you love and unselfishly seek the best for one another, just as I have loved you."

JOHN 15:9–12 AMP

Daily Choices

You have a choice every day when you wake up: you can choose to be thankful for a new day and look at it with joy and hopeful expectation, or you can choose to let the day get ahead of you and spend the rest of the day trying to catch up.

The second choice happens a lot if you aren't careful. And then, instead of looking at each moment as a gift, you are full of stress and worry.

I want to help you see each new day as a gift. When you wake up, come to Me. I will go before you and remind you that My Spirit is always with you. Start the day with thankfulness on your heart for your life and for all that you've been given. Thank Me for your health. Bring Me anything that is worrying you. Talk to Me about it all.

Are we headed to a dreaded dentist procedure today? I am with you. Got a big test? I can help you think clearly. Talk to Me in your heart and mind throughout this day, and it will make all the difference in your attitude. Choose to see each day and each moment as a gift—one that you can share with Me.

I am the God of hope. Let Me fill you with all joy and peace as you trust in Me, so that you may overflow with hope by the power of the Holy Spirit (Romans 15:13).

"When a woman gives birth, she has a hard time, there's no getting around it. But when the baby is born, there is joy in the birth. This new life in the world wipes out memory of the pain. The sadness you have right now is similar to that pain, but the coming joy is also similar. When I see you again, you'll be full of joy, and it will be a joy no one can rob from you. You'll no longer be so full of questions. This is what I want you to do: Ask the Father for whatever is in keeping with the things I've revealed to you. Ask in my name, according to my will, and he'll most certainly give it to you. Your joy will be a river overflowing its banks!"

JOHN 16:21–24 MSG

Finding Joy

I promise to fill you with My joy, and you don't have to wait until heaven for that! Look at what the psalmist wrote in Psalm 16:11 (NIV): "You make known to me the path of life; you will fill me with joy in your presence, with eternal pleasures at your right hand."

You can count on that, child! You have access to My peace, joy, grace, and presence right now while you live on earth—it's through the power of My Holy Spirit.

You know I went through darkness, betrayal, weakness, torture, and death on earth. Take this in: "He's been through weakness and testing, experienced it all—all but the sin. So let's walk right up to him and get what he is so ready to give" (Hebrews 4:15–16 MSG).

It's true. I went through more than you could imagine so My love would be known to the world. And because I've experienced all that, I know exactly how you feel. So you can draw near to Me, and I will fill you with peace and joy in My presence. That's My power at work in your life.

I want you to know and believe that I am with you in this very moment. If you're having trouble feeling joy in your life, get alone with Me and let's talk. Tell Me exactly how you feel—either out loud, in your mind, or jotted down in a journal. I want you to have joy in your heart. And if you don't, let Me help!

"But now I am coming to You; and I say these things [while I am still] in the world so that they may experience My joy made full and complete and perfect within them [filling their hearts with My delight]. I have given to them Your word [the message You gave Me]; and the world has hated them because they are not of the world and do not belong to the world, just as I am not of the world and do not belong to it. I do not ask You to take them out of the world, but that You keep them and protect them from the evil one. They are not of the world, just as I am not of the world."

JOHN 17:13–16 AMP

My Prayer for You

My disciples were sad that I was going to leave them. John 17 records the prayer that I prayed for Myself, for My disciples, and for *you*. Yes, I was praying for you way back then too! You have *always* been on My mind. I prayed that the same love God the Father has for Me would be in you. I want you to know and live in My love.

My disciples didn't understand that when I went back to heaven, I would send My Spirit to live in their hearts. They didn't understand that I would be alive in them. It was a great mystery until they experienced the gift of My Holy Spirit for themselves.

When I was on earth, I had limits because I was in a human body. I couldn't be everywhere all at once. My body got tired just like yours does. I needed rest and food for energy. Now that I've risen and conquered death, My Spirit can be everywhere—at all times. See here: "God decided to let his people know this rich and glorious truth which he has for all people. This truth is Christ himself, who is in you. He is our only hope for glory" (Colossians 1:27 ICB).

I am the hope of the world. And My Spirit is alive in you. You are *never* alone. You are *never* without My power at work in you. I love you.

"I do not pray for these followers only. I pray for those who will put their trust in Me through the teaching they have heard. May they all be as one, Father, as You are in Me and I am in You. May they belong to Us. Then the world will believe that You sent Me. I gave them the honor You gave Me that they may be one as We are One. I am in them and You are in Me so they may be one and be made perfect. Then the world may know that You sent Me and that You love them as You love Me. Father, I want My followers You gave Me to be with Me where I am. Then they may see My shining-greatness which You gave Me because You loved Me before the world was made."

JOHN 17:20–24 NLV

Service, Faith, and Love

I have given all My followers work to do here on earth—while you wait for Me to come back and set up the new heaven and the new earth. I've given each of My children special gifts and talents to use in serving Me and sharing My love with others. I don't want My children to be lazy. I'm always here to give you energy and purpose as you walk with Me.

I can give you strength to be faithful—to do what you say you're going to do! As you're faithful in small things, I'll give you bigger and bigger opportunities. I will continue to mold you into the young woman I created you to be. You will make a difference in the world, child!

I know that humans easily lose interest in a job once they become stuck or bored. Finishing a job requires patience, stamina, and faithfulness. I can give you all those things. I can help you finish the job well—if you depend on Me.

Galatians 5:6 (NIV) is a good verse to remember: "The only thing that counts is faith expressing itself through love." So if you're feeling tired and weak, remember that I will be your strength for you. I can help you love like I love.

Just like I sent My disciples, I am sending you out into the world as My representative. Have faith in Me. Share My love.

So when it was evening on that same day, the first day of the week, though the disciples were [meeting] behind barred doors for fear of the Jews, Jesus came and stood among them, and said, "Peace to you." After He said this, He showed them His hands and His side. When the disciples saw the Lord, they were filled with great joy. Then Jesus said to them again, "Peace to you; as the Father has sent Me, I also send you [as My representatives]." And when He said this, He breathed on them and said to them, "Receive the Holy Spirit. If you forgive the sins of anyone they are forgiven [because of their faith]; if you retain the sins of anyone, they are retained [and remain unforgiven because of their unbelief]."

JOHN 20:19–23 AMP

Faith in the Unseen

Thomas was one of My original twelve disciples. He was with Me during My ministry on earth, and yet he still had a difficult time believing I rose from the dead—even after witnessing many of My miracles firsthand! (Adults have a hard time believing in miracles sometimes.)

I knew that Thomas needed to see My scars for him to believe, so I went to him. I showed him My scars up close. I allowed him to touch Me and see for himself.

I know My followers often wish I had never left the earth. They wish I was still with them in bodily form. But take note of My words to Thomas in today's verse: "Because you have seen me, you have believed; blessed are those who have not seen and yet have believed."

I'm talking about you, dear one—and everyone who would come to believe in Me after I went back to heaven. Even better blessings are in store for those who believe without seeing. Here's why: "But I tell you the truth, it is to your advantage that I go away; for if I do not go away, the Helper (Comforter, Advocate, Intercessor—Counselor, Strengthener, Standby) will not come to you; but if I go, I will send Him (the Holy Spirit) to you [to be in close fellowship with you]" (John 16:7 AMP).

If I hadn't left, My Spirit wouldn't have come to live in the hearts of all who believe. My Spirit—alive and in the hearts of all My people—is able to accomplish everything.

So the other disciples told him, "We have seen the Lord!"
But he said to them, "Unless I see the nail marks in his
hands and put my finger where the nails were, and put
my hand into his side, I will not believe." A week later his
disciples were in the house again, and Thomas was with
them. Though the doors were locked, Jesus came and stood
among them and said, "Peace be with you!" Then he said
to Thomas, "Put your finger here; see my hands. Reach
out your hand and put it into my side. Stop doubting and
believe." Thomas said to him, "My Lord and my God!"
Then Jesus told him, "Because you have seen
me, you have believed; blessed are those who
have not seen and yet have believed."

JOHN 20:25–29 NIV

Your Calling

When you accept My call on your life, I bless you with divine gifts and surprises! As you'll see in today's scripture, Paul said that his life's work was to help people understand and respond to the gospel. Paul didn't feel qualified or equipped either, and the fact that I called him to do this was a real surprise—and a gift—to Paul.

You may feel like you've been put in a position that calls for more than your natural abilities, just like Paul. But when that happens, My power shows up big-time! I often call My followers to do things that are outside their comfort zone. I do this so that you will rely on My power in your life instead of counting on your own strength. When I stretch you like this, I always provide the tools you need to succeed.

Think about the gifts and talents I've given you. Can you use them to show others how much I love them? Don't be shy. I am the one who gave you your talent. When you use it with thanksgiving, you're honoring Me. Trust that I will handle all the details when I stretch you.

Bring your insecurities to Me. Let Me speak words of comfort to you. You are right where I've placed you *for a reason*—with all the gifts and abilities I've given you *for a reason*. Leave it all to Me. The details will come together in My timing.

This is my life work: helping people understand and respond to this Message. It came as a sheer gift to me, a real surprise, God handling all the details. When it came to presenting the Message to people who had no background in God's way, I was the least qualified of any of the available Christians. God saw to it that I was equipped, but you can be sure that it had nothing to do with my natural abilities. And so here I am, preaching and writing about things that are way over my head, the inexhaustible riches and generosity of Christ. My task is to bring out in the open and make plain what God, who created all this in the first place, has been doing in secret and behind the scenes all along. Through followers of Jesus like yourselves gathered in churches, this extraordinary plan of God is becoming known and talked about even among the angels!

EPHESIANS 3:7–10 MSG

Blessings

My blessings can be witnessed throughout the entire Bible. I blessed people. And people blessed Me. And leaders often blessed their followers. Asking for My blessing is asking for My purpose and power in your life—it's not asking Me to give you everything you want. Where do you need Me to bless your life? Talk to Me about it today.

Psalm 103:1–2 (AMP) says: "Bless and affectionately praise the LORD, O my soul, and all that is [deep] within me, bless His holy name. Bless and affectionately praise the LORD, O my soul, and do not forget any of His benefits." Think about ways that you can bless Me, dear one. I love to hear your praises!

In Matthew 5:3–12, I talk about how to be blessed in My kingdom. My ways are not the ways of the world. It's an upside-down kingdom. What men view as important is counted as loss in My kingdom. As you read through today's scripture, what thoughts come to mind? Tell Me how you're doing in these areas. Where do you need My help? Think about any struggles you have and ask for My blessing. I am with you in the struggle.

I want you to see My purpose and power in your world. I want to bless your calling and show you the path I have laid out for you. My heart longs to bless you with My peace and presence.

"God blesses those who are poor and realize their need for him, for the Kingdom of Heaven is theirs. God blesses those who mourn, for they will be comforted. God blesses those who are humble, for they will inherit the whole earth. God blesses those who hunger and thirst for justice, for they will be satisfied. God blesses those who are merciful, for they will be shown mercy. God blesses those whose hearts are pure, for they will see God. God blesses those who work for peace, for they will be called the children of God. God blesses those who are persecuted for doing right, for the Kingdom of Heaven is theirs."

MATTHEW 5:3–10 NLT

Power in My Name

Through the power of My Spirit, Peter healed a poor man who had a disability from birth that prevented him from walking. The man jumped to his feet and began praising God. All the people around were astonished and went running to them. Peter asked them why they were all surprised at the man's healing. Hadn't they been listening? Peter and John had been telling them all about what I had done and My power that was available to those who believed. The man was healed through faith in My name.

Remember, My name is very powerful, dear one. No one should use My name lightly. It's not a magic word; and it should never be used in vain. Here's a great truth to remember: "There is salvation in no one else, for there is no other name under heaven given among men by which we must be saved" (Acts 4:12 ESV).

You can say My name out loud as a prayer anytime, and I will hear you. My disciples found out how powerful My name was: "The seventy-two returned with joy, saying, 'Lord, even the demons are subject to us in your name!' And he said to them, '. . .Do not rejoice in this, that the spirits are subject to you, but rejoice that your names are written in heaven'" (Luke 10:17–18, 20 ESV).

Yes, My name has power, but remember to use it wisely in prayer—with honor—knowing that the power comes from Me.

Now a man who was lame from birth was being carried to the temple gate called Beautiful, where he was put every day to beg from those going into the temple courts. When he saw Peter and John about to enter, he asked them for money. Peter looked straight at him, as did John. Then Peter said, "Look at us!" So the man gave them his attention, expecting to get something from them. Then Peter said, "Silver or gold I do not have, but what I do have I give you. In the name of Jesus Christ of Nazareth, walk." Taking him by the right hand, he helped him up, and instantly the man's feet and ankles became strong. He jumped to his feet and began to walk. Then he went with them into the temple courts, walking and jumping, and praising God. . . . "By faith in the name of Jesus, this man whom you see and know was made strong. It is Jesus' name and the faith that comes through him that has completely healed him, as you can all see."

ACTS 3:2–8, 16 NIV

Have You Been with Me?

My friends Peter and John were speaking to the people of Israel. This was after I had gone back to heaven. They were obeying My command to go and tell the world about Me. Peter and John weren't educated men—they were simple fishermen who had chosen to follow Me. But they were courageous because they knew Me personally. The people knew by their words and actions that they must have been given supernatural power. They could tell that Peter and John had been with Me!

Do you think people can tell when you've been with Me? Does your friendship with Me make a difference in your life and in your relationships? I want that for you. You are My ambassador, My representative on earth. I want you to take My message of love and salvation to the people I place in your life.

Psalm 73:28 (NIV) says: "But as for me, it is good to be near God. I have made the Sovereign LORD my refuge." It's good to be near Me. I am your refuge—a safe place. Come to Me for protection, relief, and escape. When you make Me your refuge, it means you trust Me to meet all your needs. You talk to Me about everything. You listen for My voice in your life.

When you do this every day, everyone around you will be able to tell that you've been with Me!

Then Peter, filled with the Holy Spirit, said to them: "Rulers and elders of the people! If we are being called to account today for an act of kindness shown to a man who was lame and are being asked how he was healed, then know this, you and all the people of Israel: It is by the name of Jesus Christ of Nazareth, whom you crucified but whom God raised from the dead, that this man stands before you healed. Jesus is 'the stone you builders rejected, which has become the cornerstone.' Salvation is found in no one else, for there is no other name under heaven given to mankind by which we must be saved." When they saw the courage of Peter and John and realized that they were unschooled, ordinary men, they were astonished and they took note that these men had been with Jesus.

ACTS 4:8–13 NIV

My Influence in Your Heart

My followers were under attack, just as I had warned them. My friends were on trial for spreading the gospel to everyone who would listen. The authorities had told them to stop; but My followers knew the truth about My power and My salvation, and they would not stop sharing the truth. They knew that they had to obey Me instead of the government authorities.

When you stay in constant connection with Me, our relationship grows and thrives. But when you spend too much time with others and stop thinking of Me throughout the day, people will start getting big and I will start getting small in your heart. That means that people will have more of an influence in your life than I do.

The approval of certain people might seem super important to you. You want your teacher or coach or friends to like you. But they might all be telling you one thing, when you know in your heart that I need you to do something else. It's much more important to obey and follow Me than it is to please any person.

I will always give you the strength to say the right thing at the right time and to do what I am asking you to do. If I am feeling too small in your heart and mind, and people seem too big, then talk to Me about it, dear one. I gave My disciples courage and power through My Spirit; they were able to stand up for their faith even under severe attack. And I will help you too.

They brought the missionaries in and made them stand in front of the court. The head religious leader said, "We told you not to teach about Christ! See! You are spreading this teaching over all Jerusalem. Now you are making it look as if we are guilty of killing this Man." Then Peter and the missionaries said, "We must obey God instead of men! The God of our early fathers raised up Jesus, the One you killed and nailed to a cross. God raised this Man to His own right side as a leader and as the One Who saves from the punishment of sin. He makes it possible for the Jews to be sorry for their sins. Then they can turn from them and be forgiven. We have seen these things and are telling about them. The Holy Spirit makes these things known also. God gives His Spirit to those who obey Him."

ACTS 5:27–32 NLV

A Mountain of Problems

Imagine you are an early settler in America. Your family is traveling west to meet up with family who have gone before you. You've been on the wagon train for weeks and weeks. And suddenly, you go over the next hill and a large mountain is standing in your way. How will you ever get across? When you are staring at a large, steep mountain in the distance, knowing you need to reach the top to resolve an issue, things can seem big and scary and hopeless. But what if you get closer to the mountain and see that a small, smooth path circles around it—all the way to the other side? You discover that you were worried and stressed for nothing!

Your problems can seem just like that, right? I want you to learn to bring all your anxiety and fears to Me. I will help make your path smooth.

My friend Isaiah wrote this: "But for those who are righteous, the way is not steep and rough. You are a God who does what is right, and you smooth out the path ahead of them. LORD, we show our trust in you by obeying your laws; our heart's desire is to glorify your name" (Isaiah 26:7–8 NLT).

Can you learn to trust Me like that? I am your righteousness; and I'm the one who makes you righteous, so this scripture is true for you as well. As you follow Me and stick close to Me, I can make your mountain of problems turn into a smooth, easily travelable path.

He didn't tiptoe around God's promise asking cautiously skeptical questions. He plunged into the promise and came up strong, ready for God, sure that God would make good on what he had said. That's why it is said, "Abraham was declared fit before God by trusting God to set him right." But it's not just Abraham; it's also us! The same thing gets said about us when we embrace and believe the One who brought Jesus to life when the conditions were equally hopeless. The sacrificed Jesus made us fit for God, set us right with God.

ROMANS 4:20–25 MSG

Caterpillars and Transformation

When Moses met with God the Father in the Old Testament, it transformed everything about him. Even his skin was glowing with the radiance of God's glory—so much that Moses had to wear a veil so people wouldn't be afraid to come near him.

Because of My work on the cross, making a way for *all* people to come to God, I removed the veil that comes between God and mankind. Without Me, a veil would still cover your heart, preventing you from seeing and hearing from God.

When you experience Me face-to-face, I transform you into My image. Every day that you spend with Me, you start looking a little more like Me. As you grow up, you are being transformed in many ways. You're changing from being a child—transforming little by little into the young woman I designed you to be. I want to re-create and renew every thought and action you have, dear one.

Growing up and transforming can be a frustrating process, but don't let it get you down. I have purpose for all things. A caterpillar must stop eating, hang upside down, and spin itself into a cocoon where the metamorphosis occurs before it can become a butterfly. Aren't you glad you don't have to do that to become a woman?

When you come face-to-face with Me every day, there is

freedom and love and help for your transformation process. I am preparing you to fly!

Therefore, since we have such a hope, we are very bold. We are not like Moses, who would put a veil over his face to prevent the Israelites from seeing the end of what was passing away. But their minds were made dull, for to this day the same veil remains when the old covenant is read. It has not been removed, because only in Christ is it taken away. Even to this day when Moses is read, a veil covers their hearts. But whenever anyone turns to the Lord, the veil is taken away. Now the Lord is the Spirit, and where the Spirit of the Lord is, there is freedom. And we all, who with unveiled faces contemplate the Lord's glory, are being transformed into his image with ever-increasing glory, which comes from the Lord, who is the Spirit.

2 CORINTHIANS 3:12–18 NIV

Expecting Joy and Troubles

I know that life on earth can be very difficult. I see it all, dear one. Trouble will come. But so will joy. Therefore, take heart! I have overcome the world (John 16:33). I want to talk with you about living with joy in your heart, even while expecting that trouble will come. I do not want you to be paranoid, always expecting bad things and holding fear in your heart. No—exactly the opposite. I want you to wake up each morning expecting some challenges but knowing I will be with you through every one!

A prayer of "Lord, I'm thankful for a new day. How are You and I going to handle the challenges we face today?" is a great way to start your day with Me. Instead of waking up grumpy or afraid, let Me take your hand as we solve all your problems *together*. I even promise to fill your heart with joy as we do it! There is *always* joy in My presence.

I don't want you to wake up expecting the worst, because I can always take what the enemy meant for evil and use it for good (Genesis 50:20). Begin to look at trouble as a challenge that can be conquered with My power alive and at work in you.

When trouble comes, you are sharing in My sufferings. My Spirit is resting on you and living in you—giving you strength, joy, and courage as you live this adventurous life.

Beloved, do not be surprised at the fiery ordeal which is taking place to test you [that is, to test the quality of your faith], as though something strange or unusual were happening to you. But insofar as you are sharing Christ's sufferings, keep on rejoicing, so that when His glory [filled with His radiance and splendor] is revealed, you may rejoice with great joy. If you are insulted and reviled for [bearing] the name of Christ, you are blessed [happy, with life-joy and comfort in God's salvation regardless of your circumstances], because the Spirit of glory and of God is resting on you [and indwelling you—He whom they curse, you glorify].

1 PETER 4:12–14 AMP

217

A Much-Needed Reminder

The love I have for you is like no other love, dear one. My love is unfailing and faithful. I will never let you down. I am always here for you. I am listening, and I love you like you're the only girl in the whole world. You are My child, and you are precious to Me. I have so many wonderful plans for your life. Even the painful things that happen, I will miraculously turn into good things—if you trust in Me. I began a good work in you, and I will continue that work until it's finished on the day I return (Philippians 1:6).

As you continue to mature into a young woman, you're going to meet a lot of distractions that compete for your attention. These distractions will try to get you to turn away from trusting in My great love for you. The enemy continues to prowl around looking for someone he can devour and turn away from Me. Resist him. Put on your spiritual armor; keep telling him the truth by hiding My Word in your heart; and then you'll win those battles with My strength.

Keep coming to Me, friend. Seek Me, and you'll find Me. Keep your eyes and heart focused on My great love for you. Keep bringing all your thoughts and feelings to Me every day—and we will sort them all out *together*. I have unlimited power, and I want to bless you with peace and joy in My presence.

O Lord, all the kings of the earth will give thanks to You when they have heard the words of Your mouth. And they will sing of the ways of the Lord. For the shining beauty of the Lord is great. For even if the Lord is honored, He thinks about those who have no pride. But He knows the proud from far away. Even if I walk into trouble, You will keep my life safe. You will put out Your hand against the anger of those who hate me. And Your right hand will save me. The Lord will finish the work He started for me. O Lord, Your loving-kindness lasts forever. Do not turn away from the works of Your hands.

PSALM 138:4–8 NLV

Your Commission

Right before I went back to heaven, I spoke some powerful words to My followers. I commissioned them to go into the world and tell others about Me—baptizing them and teaching them how to live according to My ways. I reminded them of My power and gave them a plan of action. The disciples knew that My power was real, and so they went and did as I asked. They knew I conquered death because they saw it all happen. Everything that I said would take place happened. They knew I could offer hope and healing to the most broken people. They knew I was the way to eternal life. They shared about Me everywhere they went, and the gospel was made known worldwide. Because of the faithfulness of My followers through the ages, the good news is still being shared today.

Just like I commissioned My disciples, I am commissioning you. The mission is yours now—and it's the same as it's always been, if you choose to accept it. The power of My Spirit lives inside you, and I'm authorizing you to take My power and share My story of love and hope with the world. You'll have many chances to share My light and love with others just by being you. My power is at work in you, and you are set apart for a reason.

Go into the world and share courageously, dear one. I am with you always.

Now the eleven disciples went to Galilee, to the mountain which Jesus had designated. And when they saw Him, they worshiped Him; but some doubted [that it was really He]. Jesus came up and said to them, "All authority (all power of absolute rule) in heaven and on earth has been given to Me. Go therefore and make disciples of all the nations [help the people to learn of Me, believe in Me, and obey My words], baptizing them in the name of the Father and of the Son and of the Holy Spirit, teaching them to observe everything that I have commanded you; and lo, I am with you always [remaining with you perpetually—regardless of circumstance, and on every occasion], even to the end of the age."
MATTHEW 28:16–20 AMP

Trust in My Word

Part of trusting Me is trusting in the truth of My Word. I want you to know and believe that the Bible is My inspired Word. Remember this: "All Scripture is God-breathed [given by divine inspiration] and is profitable for instruction, for conviction [of sin], for correction [of error and restoration to obedience], for training in righteousness. . .so that the man of God may be complete and proficient, outfitted and thoroughly equipped for every good work" (2 Timothy 3:16–17 AMP).

Don't be afraid to search out the truth for yourself. I want you to truly understand what you believe and why you believe it. I want you to always be prepared to share with others when they ask about the hope you have (1 Peter 3:15).

As strange as this might sound, many people have come to know Me by trying to prove the Bible wrong! Remember, My Word is alive and active. Science and history and archaeology have all confirmed that the Bible is true. Rulers, kings, and countries have tried to ban My Word for generations, and yet it remains. My Word cannot be destroyed. It will always accomplish what I desire (Isaiah 55:11).

My Word can be trusted. If you want to know how to live your life for Me. . . If you need wisdom for today and hope for tomorrow. . . If you want to hear Me speak to you right now. . . Get in My Word. It *will* change your life!

Jesus said to him, "Because you have seen Me, do you now believe? Blessed [happy, spiritually secure, and favored by God] are they who did not see [Me] and yet believed [in Me]." There are also many other signs (attesting miracles) that Jesus performed in the presence of the disciples, which are not written in this book; but these have been written so that you may believe [with a deep, abiding trust] that Jesus is the Christ (the Messiah, the Anointed), the Son of God; and that by believing [and trusting in and relying on Him] you may have life in His name.

JOHN 20:29–31 AMP

More Inspiration for Your Heart

You Matter

This delightful devotional, created just for teen girls like you,
is a beautiful reminder of your purpose. . .your worth. . .your
place in the world. 180 encouraging readings and inspiring
prayers, rooted in biblical truth, will reassure your doubting
heart. In each devotional reading, you will encounter the
bountiful love and grace of your Creator, while coming to
understand His plan—for you and you alone.

Flexible Casebound / 978-1-64352-520-4